DESIGN!

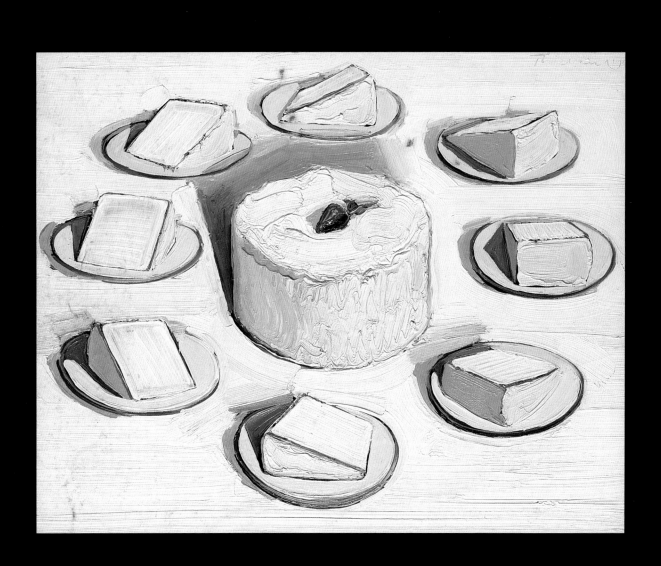

DESIGN!
A Lively Guide to Design Basics for Artists & Craftspeople

Steven Aimone

LARK BOOKS

A Division of Sterling Publishing Co., Inc.
New York

Editor: **PAIGE GILCHRIST**

Art Director: **DANA M. IRWIN**

Cover Designer: **BARBARA ZARETSKY**

Illustrator: **DANA M. IRWIN**

Associate Editor: **VERONIKA ALICE GUNTER**

Assistant Editor: **NATHALIE MORNU**

Production Assistance: **HANNES CHAREN, AVERY JOHNSON, LANCE WILLE, SHANNON YOKELEY**

Editorial Assistance: **DELORES GOSNELL, ROSEMARY KAST, RAIN NEWCOMB**

Interns: **ROBIN HEIMER, REBECCA LIM**

Credits for imagery on the cover and the half title, title, and dedication pages and the table of contents appear on page 175.

The Library of Congress had cataloged the hardcover edition as follows:

Aimone, Steven.
  Design! : a lively guide to design basics for artists & craftspeople /
by Steven Aimone.
      p. cm.
Includes index.
  ISBN 1-57990-349-5 (hard cover)
  1. Design—Technique. I. Title.
  NK1510.G49 2004
  745.4—dc22

                                        2003015805

10 9 8 7 6 5 4 3 2 1

Published by Lark Books, a division of
Sterling Publishing Co., Inc.
387 Park Avenue South, New York, N.Y. 10016

First Paperback Edition 2007
© 2004, Steven Aimone

Distributed in Canada by Sterling Publishing,
c/o Canadian Manda Group, 165 Dufferin Street
Toronto, Ontario, Canada M6K 3H6

Distributed in the United Kingdom by GMC Distribution Services,
Castle Place, 166 High Street, Lewes, East Sussex, England BN7 1XU

Distributed in Australia by Capricorn Link (Australia) Pty Ltd.,
P.O. Box 704, Windsor, NSW 2756 Australia

If you have questions or comments about this book, please contact:
Lark Books
67 Broadway
Asheville, NC 28801
(828) 253-0467
Printed in China

ISBN 13: 978-1-57990-349-7 (hardcover) 978-1-60059-136-5 (paperback)
ISBN 10: 1-57990-349-5 (hardcover) 1-60059-136-1 (paperback)

For information about custom editions, special sales, premium and corporate purchases, please contact Sterling Special Sales Department at 800-805-5489 or specialsales@sterlingpub.com.

TO MY WIFE KATHERINE.
YOU ARE MY SUNSHINE...

CONTENTS

INTRODUCTION

Want to learn more about design? Simply stop and take a look at the world around you. This book will open your eyes and show you how.

Maybe you're a craftsperson or artist who hopes to expand your awareness and ability. Or, perhaps you're a Sunday museum-goer who wants to further your appreciation and enjoyment of art and craft. Whatever your reason for reading this book it's an exciting and accessible introduction to design that will help you understand basic concepts and create your own effective designs.

Design is something you encounter everywhere, every day of your life. You see it in the shape and color of a street sign, the woven details of a basket, the arrangement of food on a plate, the colors in a window display, or the texture of a crocheted hat. Whether you're aware of it or not, you're also constantly designing, even when doing something as simple as arranging furniture, stacking wood, or setting a table.

In other words, you already have some sense of design, and you don't need any formal training or experience in the subject to use this book to the fullest. You'll be able to follow its simple step-by-step approach to gain the skills you need to put the concepts to work. If you already have a background as a designer, artist, or craftsperson, you'll be

Stop Sign, 2003
Photo by Sandra Stambaugh;
immediate right.

HELGA MEYER, *Mask,* 1995.
Papier-mâché mask from clay form.
Photo by Hayo Heye; top.

CYNTHIA W. TAYLOR, *Egg Basket with Side Handles,* 2000. 7 ¼ x 13 ½ x 11 ½ inches (18.4 x 34.3 x 29.2 cm). Handsplit white oak.
Photo © 2000 by Paul Jeremias; middle.

BARBARA ZARETSKY, *Hat,* 2002. 5 x 9 x 9 inches (13 x 23 x 23 cm). Crocheted wool with silk edge.
Photo by Tim Barnwell; bottom.

DALE BROHOLM, *Writer's Cabinet,* 2002. 76 x 20 x14 inches (193 x 50.8 x 35.6 cm). Curly ash veneer, solid ebony, paper. *Photo by Dean Powell; top left.*

CAROLINE STREEP, *Bracelet in the Galactic Voyager series,* 1990. 1 3/4 x 6 1/4 inches (4.5 x 15.9 cm). File-finished sterling silver, 18 karat gold fused with granules and gold beads, 22 karat gold stone settings, tourmaline, chalcedony, amethyst. *Photo by artist; bottom left.*

KENNETH TRUMBAUER, 2002. Floral arrangement; crespedia, vodka glasses, marbles, vodka cooler. *Art Direction by Dana Irwin, photo by Sandra Stambaugh; top middle.*

SUSIE GANCH, *Decadence,* 2001. Women's size 6. Slip cast sugar with sterling silver stiletto heels. *Photo by John Littleton; bottom middle.*

ALZIARI OLIVE OIL CAN, designed 1936. *Photo by Steve Mann. Courtesy of the Nicolas Alziari company; top right.*

YVETTE SMALLS, *Ancient Senegalese Twist,* 2002. Hair design. Model: Kim Simpkins. *Photo by Miyoshi Smith; bottom right.*

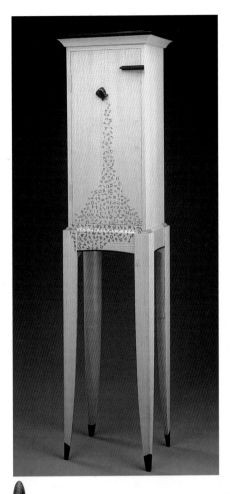

able to easily adapt the material in this book to your medium. The fundamental ideas are the same, no matter how they're applied. Whether you make quilts, paint watercolors, throw pots, create masks, build furniture, style hair, or engage in another creative activity, this book will enrich your understanding of the process.

DESIGN IS SOMETHING YOU ENCOUNTER EVERYWHERE, EVERY DAY OF YOUR LIFE.

THE SAME BASIC ELEMENTS
HAVE BEEN CONFIGURED
IN SIMILAR WAYS
THROUGHOUT TIME
AND ACROSS CULTURES,
REGARDLESS OF MEDIA.

Simply put, design is the arrangement of visual elements in a space. Everything you'll learn in this book revolves around this idea, and the process is universal. The same basic elements have been configured in similar ways throughout time and across cultures, regardless of media. Consider, for example, the striking similarities between Mozell Benson's African-American quilt, above, and Piet Mondrian's abstract painting, facing page. Although these works were created for radically different reasons in different cultures, the pieces seem like kindred spirits, both in feeling and structure.

This book's approach was developed out of my own experience teaching design workshops and courses to a wide range of people, including professional artists and craftspeople, college students, museum

MOZELL BENSON, *Strip Variation Quilt,* 1991. 89 x 70½ inches (226.1 x 179.1 cm). Cotton, wool, yarn. *Collection of the American Folk Art Museum, New York (Purchase made possible in part by a grant from the National Endowment for the Arts, with matching funds from the Great American Quilt Festival 3, accession number 1991.13.9). Photo by Scott Bowron; facing page.*

PIET MONDRIAN, *Composition with Grey, Red, Yellow, and Blue, circa 1920.* Approx. 32¾ x 33 inches (83 x 84 cm). Oil on canvas. Tate Gallery, London, Great Britain. *Photo copyright Tate Gallery, London/Art Resource, NY; left.*

patrons, and school teachers. My students learn by looking at and talking about a broad range of inspiring work before tackling hands-on challenges that put concepts into action. You'll do the same as you work your way through this book, and your knowledge will expand as you go.

Early in the book, you'll learn about different purposes of design. You'll also look closely at each of the raw materials you have to work with when you create a design: line, mark, shape/form, texture, and color. This first section of the book concludes by considering the nature and dynamics of the design space—the area that frames or contains the design elements.

In the remaining chapters, you'll explore six basic ways of organizing designs—through repetition, rhythm, symmetry, asymmetry, focal emphasis, and underlying

MATTHEW FELDMAN, *Purse,* 2001.
7 1/2 x 8 1/2 x 5 1/4 inches (19.1 x 21.6 x
13.3 cm). Leather, silver, gold, white
gold. *Photo by Clark Quin. Collection of
the Museum of Fine Arts, Boston, MA;
top right.*

CURTIS BUCHANAN,
Bird Cage Windsor, 1993.
36 x 19 x 20 inches
(91.5 x 48.3 x 50.8 cm). Oak, pine,
maple, milk paint. *Photo by Tom Pardue;
bottom right.*

PIER VOULKOS,
Shaped Beads,
1995. Approx. 24 inches (61 cm) long.
Polymer clay. *Photo by Steven Ford;
facing page, top left.*

CHARLES MANN, *York Garden Gate,*
1991. Color photograph of a garden in
West Yorkshire, England;
facing page, bottom left.

LINDA McNALLY, *Polly Gayton,*
1999. 8 x 10 inches (20.3 x 25.4 cm).
Traditional counted crossstitch.
*Photo by Matthew Thompson;
facing page, top middle.*

STARDUST NEON SIGN, 1968. 188
feet (57.3 m) tall. *Photo by Greg Cava.
Courtesy of Stardust Resort and Casino,
Las Vegas, NV; facing page, center.*

**AIRBRUSHED RESTAURANT CHINA
CUP AND SAUCER,** 1958. Commercial
vitrified china manufactured by Sterling
China. *Photo by Steve Mann.
Collection of the author;
facing page, bottom middle .*

Toaster from Universal product line,
1918-1923. Manufactured by Landers,
Frary & Clark, New Britain, CT. *Collection
of Carole and Larry Meeke;
facing page, far right.*

shapes. Each of these chapters, along with the earlier sections on color, has a three-part structure.

1. Overview: This introductory section gives you a general understanding of the concepts involved.

2. Examples: Next, we'll view and discuss a wide range of design examples that illustrate the concepts and bring them to life. You'll see, for instance, how contrasting color functions similarly in everything from ceramics to clothing. Or how a repeating motif can unify a design, whether it's in the form of a 15th-century painting, an art deco poster, or a contemporary coffeepot.

3. Exercises: Finally, exercises at the end of each section or chapter show you how to work with the concepts on your own.

In the sections on color, you'll do most of the exercises with paint, because it offers the most flexible, clear way of exploring possibilities, even if you usually work with another medium. You'll be able to easily transfer what you've learned to your favorite medium once you're familiar with the concepts. Use any paints and brushes you have on hand or can easily find, whether fine art paints or craft supplies. The exercises in later chapters use collage and stamping, two ways of working that are accessible to anyone.

The concluding chapter of the book simulates the critique portion of a workshop, analyzing various designs in a wide range of works. By this point, you'll know enough to do some critiquing yourself, and you'll likely have thoughts to add to mine. More important, you'll begin to see that when you heighten your awareness of design, you open up a world of limitless possibilities for personal enjoyment and creative expression that you can apply to all realms of your life.

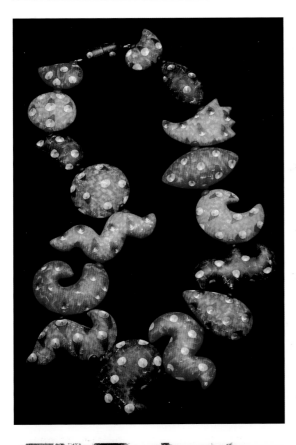

WHEN YOU
HEIGHTEN YOUR
AWARENESS OF DESIGN,
YOU OPEN UP A WORLD
OF LIMITLESS POSSIBILITIES
FOR PERSONAL ENJOYMENT
AND CREATIVE EXPRESSION

CHAPTER 1

THE PURPOSES OF DESIGN

REMBRANDT VAN RIJN,
The Syndics of the
Clothworkers' Guild, 1665.
75¼ x 199¾ inches
(191.5 x 279 cm).
Oil on canvas. *Rijksmuseum,*
Amsterdam, Holland.

RICHARD STRAUSS, *United*
States Supreme Court,
1994. Color photograph.
Collection of The Supreme
Court Historical Society.

Why create a *design*? What function can it serve? What can it express or reveal? The purposes of design fall roughly into five categories: *descriptive* (to document the visible world), *narrative* (to tell a story or send a message), *emotive* (to evoke a mood), *utilitarian* (to perform a practical function), and *decorative* (to creatively arrange design elements, such as *color* and *shape*). Keep in mind that most designs serve more than one of these purposes. In fact, overlap is almost inevitable. Usually, however, one design purpose is primary, and the success of any design can be judged by how well it achieves its purpose.

DESCRIPTIVE

Have you ever taken a photograph of a place you've visited so you could share it with friends who haven't seen it? Have you posted a picture of a lost pet in hopes that somebody in the neighborhood would find it, or photographed a house in preparation for advertising it for sale? Maybe you've built a scarecrow and put it in the garden to ward off crows. In all of these cases, the primary intention is to describe or document. A descriptive design conveys the visible reality of a subject. Description is the main motivation for *documentary* photographers, portrait painters, sculptors, and illustrators. And, as suggested, we all document or describe in our everyday lives.

Before the camera became a commonly available tool, painting, drawing, and sculpture were used for documentation. If you lived in western Europe prior to photography and wanted to have your physical attributes documented, you might have hired a painter such as Rembrandt van Rijn. In *The Syndics of the Clothworkers' Guild*, facing page, top, Rembrandt painted the likenesses of six members of a local craftsman's guild, documenting their appearances and station in life. More recently, Richard Strauss documented the appearances of the members of the U.S. Supreme Court photographically, facing page, bottom.

An illustrated poster dating back to 1869, right, uses hand-drawn images to describe the wonders of the American west—and lure settlers. A century later, a state tourism organization uses documentary photography, above, to describe one of its locations, with the aim of luring vacationers.

Wendell Castle's *Ghost Clock*, right, is an example of description for its own sake. In this *trompe-l'oeil* (fool the eye) sculpture, what appears to be a grandfather clock draped in cloth is actually a piece made entirely of wood. Paul Dresang engages in the same kind of illusion, only this time in ceramics in *Untitled*, far right.

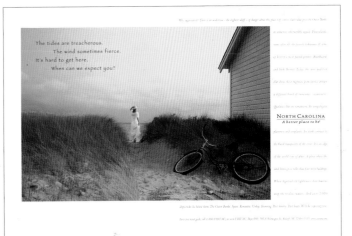

JIM MOUNTJOY (creative director), **DOUG PEDERSEN** (art director), **ED JONES** (copywriter), **HARRY DEZITTER** (photographer), *Tides,* 1993. Print advertisement. *Courtesy of North Carolina Travel & Tourism.*

ALFRED RUDOLPH WAUD, *Where to Emigrate and Why,* 1869. 8³⁄4 x 5¹⁄2 inches (22.2 x 14 cm). Wood engraving for book. *Courtesy of the Library of Congress.*

WENDELL CASTLE, *Ghost Clock,* 1985. 87¹⁄2 x 24¹⁄2 x 15 inches (222.3 x 62.3 x 38.1 cm). Bleached mahogany. *Smithsonian American Art Museum, Washington, DC/Art Resource, NY.*

PAUL DRESANG, *Untitled (Bag Form),* 1998. Approx. 20 inches (50.8 cm) long. Porcelain. *Photo by Joseph Gruber.*

GIOTTO DI BONDONE, *Scrovegni Chapel, Padua, Italy,* 1266-1336. Interior view of the chapel toward the altar. *Alinari/Art Resource, NY.*

NARRATIVE

Many designs seek to tell a story—to entertain, preach, educate, or comment. Early cave paintings were narratives about the hunt. Byzantine and Renaissance artists related stories of Christianity. Throughout history, artists have told visual stories about subjects as diverse as family history, the horrors of war, the changing seasons, and human oppression. Today, book covers and illustrations, narrative quilts, political cartoons, and conceptual art are just a few examples of designs with a narrative emphasis.

This series of fresco paintings, facing page, by the early Italian Renaissance artist Giotto, features narrative scenes from the life of Christ. Painted in four tiers, they tell the entire story, including events preceding the birth of Christ and those that happened after his death, in a clear and sequential

fashion. Similar design purposes are served in the shallow relief sculptural panels that adorn the surfaces in Nicola Pisano's *Pulpit, Baptistry (Pisa, Italy),* above right.

Continuing in this tradition, contemporary painter Gary Bolding tells the story of the life of Elvis Presley in *Elvis Mandala*, above left. His narrative functions on at least two levels. First, he tells a vivid story of Elvis's transition from boyhood through the stages of emerging rock-and-roll star, film actor, and aging performer in Las Vegas. The second narrative level is more subtle. By creating the painting in the format of a *mandala*, a ritualistic geometric design used in Hinduism and Buddhism, Bolding implies that pop stars have become our deities in contemporary culture, and he asks viewers to give that idea some thought.

GARY BOLDING, *Elvis Mandala,* 1993. 60 x 60 inches (152.4 x 152.4 cm). Oil on linen. *Collection of Hendrix College, Conway, AR.*

NICOLA PISANO, *Pulpit (Baptistry, Pisa, Italy),* c. 13th century. *Photo copyright Scala/Art Resource, NY.*

WENDY C. HUHN, *Wife Wanted,*
1996. 47 x 67 x ½ inches
(119.4 x 170.2 x 1.3 cm).
Fabrics embellished with stencils,
T-shirt transfers, screen printing,
airbrushed paint; machine quilted.
Photo by David Loveall Photography, Inc.,
Eugene, OR.

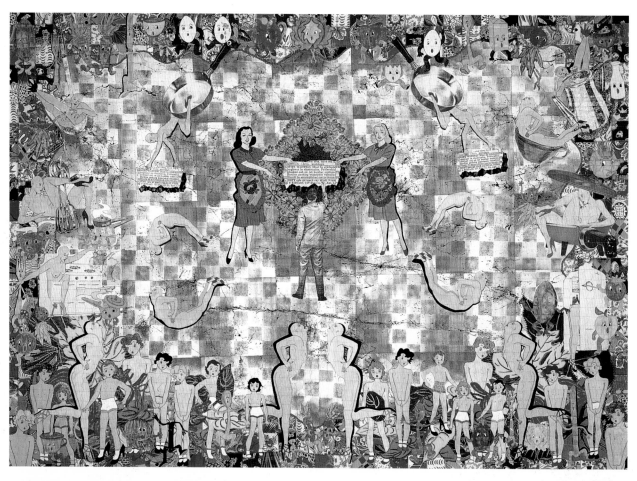

L. N. BRITTON, *Knit Your Bit,*
between 1914 and 1918. Graphic
design for American National Red
Cross and American Lithographic Co.
Courtesy of the Library of Congress.

BARBARA KRUGER, *Untitled (I*
Shop Therefore I Am), 1987.
112 x 113 inches (284.5 x 287 cm).
Photographic silkscreen on vinyl.
Private collection, courtesy Thomas
Ammann Fine Art, Zurich, Switzerland.

Textile artist Wendy C. Huhn makes an ironic narrative statement about the conflicting roles and expectations women face in *Wife Wanted*, facing page, top. Using a very traditional symmetrical design, Huhn creates a satirical ad, then offers a tongue-in-cheek response through imagery depicting women as nude, hairless creatures whose lives revolve around relationships with kitchen appliances, eggs, and vegetables.

The designer of the American National Red Cross poster, facing page, bottom left, used bold graphics in a strongly centered arrangement to urge Americans to provide troops with socks during wartime. More recently, fine artist Barbara Kruger used a similar approach in her *Untitled (I Shop Therefore I Am)*, facing page, bottom right. The screenprint on vinyl is a commentary on issues of identity in Western culture in the late 20th century.

Social commentary is an overwhelming focus of the political cartoon, as well. Garry Trudeau's narrative, above, tells of the disparity between street crime and its white collar counterpart. In a much more spontaneous and improvisational manner, graffiti artists used the Berlin Wall as a surface for their graphic protests, top.

One more narrative function of design is to promote, inform, and sell through advertisement. Harrod Blank's *Chicken Car*, right, fits this description. He's converted a luxury car into an advertisement for a fried chicken restaurant in Galliano, Louisiana.

KÄTHE KOLLWITZ, *Study for Seven Woodcuts on War: The Mothers,* about 1923. 17⅞ x 23⅛ inches (45.4 x 58.8 cm). India ink and opaque white watercolor on paper. *Museum of Fine Arts, Boston, MA (Frederick Brown Fund, accession number 55.224).*

EMOTIVE

A third purpose of design is to evoke a mood or convey a feeling. It's the overwhelming purpose of Käthe Kollwitz's brush drawing, *The Mothers,* left. She portrays a group of mothers huddled together and clutching one another out of fear and sorrow during the German depression between the World Wars.

Untitled Vessel, by Richard Zane Smith, below left, is a soft, round, beautifully distilled *form.* Its surface is highly unified by repetition of the same delicately textured shape around the form, and the colors are muted, both creating a calm feeling. Marko Fields's *Smartass Teapot Thinks It's Alive; Oughta Join the Carnival,* below right, conjures an entirely different mood. Fields infuses his design with a great deal of tension and motion. His teapot dances, gestures, and jiggles to create a playful mood. The pot tilts backwards, as if it's posturing for its audience. Its handle gyrates in an unexpected, out-of-control manner. The spout continues the line of the handle, extending up and to the right. The teapot's surface decoration, featuring an array of curved and jazzed-up shapes and colors, builds on the playful effect.

John Twachtman's *Springtime,* facing page, top left, exudes a feeling of serenity and tranquility through long horizontals; soft, muted, and cool colors; and simple, elegant shapes. Compare it to Ludwig Meidner's *Apocalyptic Landscape,* facing page, top right, and notice how radically different they

RICHARD ZANE SMITH, *Untitled Vessel,* 1991. Approx. 24 x 19 inches (61 x 48.3 cm). Native clays; built with tiny coils, shingle-lapped, stained with clay slip. *Photo by Robert Sherwood.*

MARKO FIELDS, *Smartass Teapot Thinks It's Alive; Oughta Join the Carnival,* 1997. 11 x 16 x 6 inches (27.9 x 40.6 x 15.2 cm). Porcelain, sterling silver, carnelian; thrown and altered base, slab-built top sections, bisque fired, underglaze applied and wiped off, oxidation fired, painted and sealed enamels. *Photo by artist.*

are in mood. Here, sharp diagonals reign. Lines are frenetic and jagged. Shapes are hard edged and unyielding. Almost nothing feels at rest. The arrangement is dominated by extreme darks and lights without much in between to temper the mood. While most of the painting is done in icy-cold blues, contrasting notes of red, green, and bright yellow orange bring the temperature up and increase the tension.

Compare Curtis Buchanan's *Patra's Chair*, right, and Gerald Smith's *Narrow Highback, Upholstered Seat*, far right, and you'll see the same kind of range of emotion. Buchanan's chair is elegant and balanced. Elements are arranged in *perfect symmetry*, linear movements are straight and orderly, and the spokes of its backrest create a regular and even *rhythm*. Smith's chair evokes a very different feeling. Its linear movements turn and tilt, its *symmetry* is radically tweaked, and the rhythm of its backrest is quirky and irregular, creating unusual interest and tension.

JOHN TWACHTMAN, *Springtime,* c. 1884.
36⅞ x 50 inches (93.7 x 127 cm). Oil on canvas. *The Cincinnati Art Museum, Cincinnati, OH. Gift of Frank Duveneck.*

LUDWIG MEIDNER, *Apocalyptic Landscape (Near the Halensee Railroad Station),* 1913.
37½ x 31⅝ inches (95.3 x 80.5 cm). Oil on canvas. *Los Angeles County Museum of Art, Gift of Clifford Odets.* © Ludwig Meidner-Archiv, Jüdisches Museum der Stadt Frankfurt am Main. © 2003 Museum Associates/LACMA.

CURTIS BUCHANAN, *Patra's Chair,* 1993. 38 x 22 x 20 inches (96.5 x 55.9 x 50.8 cm). Oak, poplar, maple, milk paint.
Photo by Peter Montanti.

GERALD SMITH, *Narrow High Back, Upholstered Seat,* 2001. 56 x 20 inches (30.2 x 50.8 cm). Handcrafted, refined rustic, free-form, maple narrow high back chair constructed with mortise-and-tenon joinery featuring a natural linen/cotton blend upholstered seat.
Photo by Mark Schwenk. Courtesy of Gerald Smith, Sleepywood Rustic Furniture.

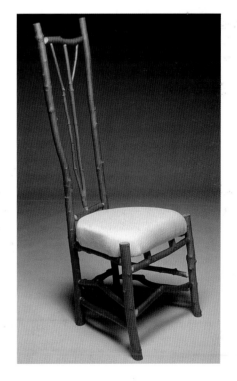

KATHRAN SIEGEL,
*Queen Ann with Blunted
Green Triangle,* 1991.
43 x 32 x 28 inches
(109.2 x 81.3 x 71.1 cm).
Carved maple, acrylic paint,
hand-dyed silk. *Photo by artist.*

JULIE MORRINGELLO,
Emoticon Screen, 1996.
5 feet 6 inches x 5 feet x 2 feet 6
inches (4.95 x 4.5 x 2.25 m).
Stencil and paint on translucent
plastic; hand fabricated stainless
steel hardware, mortised and
tenoned wood structure.
Photo by Mark Johnston.

UTILITARIAN

Furniture designers, architects, and jewelers are just a few of the designers who make items meant to be used and worn. But most such designers are no less concerned with the *aesthetics* of their pieces.

To serve as a utilitarian object, Kathran Siegel's chair *Queen Ann with Blunted Green Triangle*, above left, must support the weight of a person. If it's to function well, it should do so comfortably, meaning nonfunctional design elements shouldn't interfere with the piece's practical purpose. Siegel's design fits the requirements. Its sculptural embellishments and surface decoration are consistent with the chair's practical purpose of providing a place to sit. At the same time, the design is clearly much more than *functional*. The curvy zigzag on the right edge of the central backrest serves no practical purpose; it's just surprising and playful. In response, Siegel also emphasizes the *edges* of the chair's front feet. The swirling, circular hand rests do more than support; they complement hints of circularity throughout the design. The small triangle at the top of the backrest and the

squareness of the seat lend angular contrast to the mostly circular design features. The colors also add a lively contrast to the warmth of the unpainted wood.

Similarly, Julie Morringello's *Emoticon Screen*, above right, is utilitarian as well as narrative and decorative. The screen's purpose is to divide or section off space, which means it must stand upright. But Morringello had a lot more than this in mind. The design's surface decoration consists of typographical symbols. Narratively, the artist is asking viewers to consider the decorative potential of these recently developed symbols that represent language.

Hotel proprietors select linens, china, and flatware that are highly durable in terms of material and construction. They know that to function well, they must withstand heavy use. Some proprietors, including those at The Inn on Biltmore Estate in Asheville, North Carolina, insist that utilitarian items function decoratively and narratively as well, with the Inn logo adorning each piece, facing page, bottom left.

At first glance, the functional purpose of Fred Fenster's *Salt and Pepper*, facing page, top, can be hard to discern. What looks like a pair of distilled organic forms that relate to each other by interlocking to create a larger form is actually a functional set of pewter shakers. Fenster camouflages the utilitarian purpose of the pieces, emphasizing a sculptural look, and form and function complement one another beautifully. But if the pieces weren't hollow and didn't feature tiny holes at the top, Fenster's design, no matter how interesting to look at, would fall short of its utilitarian purpose.

The design of the Apple iMac computer, middle right, is intricately functional. Its form serves both as a container for the hardware inside and as an object for users to work with comfortably and effectively. But it also makes a bold decorative statement. When it was first released, its organic, sculptural form stood in stark contrast to the box-like forms of its competitors. Its silhouette has quickly become a cultural icon.

Finally, in a highly controversial departure from conventional museum design, the interior of Frank Lloyd Wright's Guggenheim Museum in New York, bottom right, accomplishes a utilitarian purpose in a new way. It features a long, spiraling ramp that ascends from street level to the top in one continuous movement. Viewers are able to take in an exhibition without having to move from room to room; they can gaze across the cylindrical interior to look back at works and ahead at others.

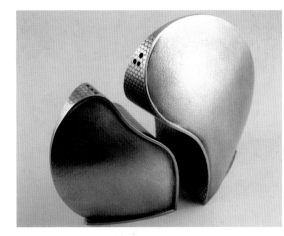

FRED FENSTER, *Salt and Pepper,* 2002. 4 ¾ inches (12.1 cm). Fabrication using pewter. *Photo by artist.*

iMac, introduced 1998. Approx. 15 ¾ x 15 x 17 ½ inches (40 x 38.1 x 44.5 cm). Desktop computer. *Photo by Hunter Freemen. Courtesy of Apple Computer. © Apple.*

Toiletries from The Inn on Biltmore Estate, 2003. *Photo by keithwright.com. Used with permission from The Biltmore Company, Asheville, NC.*

FRANK LLOYD WRIGHT, ***The Solomon R. Guggenheim Museum,*** New York, inaugurated 1959. *Photograph by David Heald © The Solomon R. Guggenheim Foundation, New York, NY.*

CHRIS SIMONCELLI, *Platter,*
2001. 23 inches (58.4 cm) in
diameter. Wheel-thrown
stoneware clay with painted
glaze; fired to cone 6.
Photo by artist.

PIET MONDRIAN,
Composition with Red,
Yellow, and Blue, 1921.
15½ x 13¾ inches
(39 x 35 cm). Oil on canvas.
Copyright Giraudon/Art Resource,
NY. Private collection, New York, NY.

DEBORA MUHL,
Orbital #1125, 2001.
11 x 12 x 9 inches
(28 x 30.5 x 22.9 cm).
Coiled basketry.
Photo by John Sterling Ruth.
Courtesy of Thirteen Moons Gallery,
Santa Fe, NM.

DECORATIVE

If you eliminate all the other purposes of design, what are you left with? A design that's simply about the creative arrangement of design elements, such as shape, color, line, *mark*, and texture. In crafts and applied arts, this purpose is referred to as decorative. It's the primary purpose for contemporary ceramist Chris Simoncelli in *Platter*, above left, where he creates a dialogue among *visual elements*. Nothing from the visible world is described, no story told, and no message sent. Instead, the surface decoration speaks for itself—a series of rounded shapes of color.

In fine art, this decorative purpose is typically called *formal* design, but it's essentially the same thing. Dutch painter Piet Mondrian was one of the founders of the approach. In a radical departure from the traditions of his time, he created arrangements that refer to nothing in the external world. Instead, they were intended to be primarily objects of meditation. *Composition with Red, Yellow, and Blue*, above right, consists of primary colors and black and white contained in rectangles and squares arranged asymmetrically. The relationships among the elements are the subject of the design. Many designers who work in this way believe such arrangements offer access to matters spiritual and transcendental.

DON GUREWITZ,
Camel Fair, 1992.
Color photograph taken
in Nagaur, India.
Collection of the artist.

LARRY HOPKINS, *Relativity,*
2000. Hair design. Model:
Valarie Carmody. *Photo by Jeff
Roth. Courtesy of Ananda Hair
Studio, Asheville, NC.*

GIORGIO MORANDI,
Still Life, 1968.
10 x 16 inches
(25.4 x 40.6 cm).
Oil on canvas.
*Photo by Steve Tatum.
Courtesy of University of Iowa
Museum of Art, Iowa City, IA.
(Gift of Owen and Leone Elliott,
accession number 1968.36.)*

In *Orbital #1125*, facing page, bottom, Debora Muhl uses the traditional materials and methods of basketmaking to create a piece that isn't functional but purely decorative. Made of sweet grass, the basket consists of a series of looping, circular repetitions in space.

The works of mid-20th-century painter Giorgio Morandi are wonderful examples of still-life paintings with a formal emphasis, middle right. Throughout his career, Morandi painted the same series of bottles, jars, jugs, and other objects, which serve as design elements to be arranged and rearranged. The distilled forms push and pull in relation to one another, creating an exciting series of relationships and tensions. In Morandi's *compositions*, apparently meaningless objects are arranged so they stand as surrogates for human relationships and emotions.

The rural people of the Nagaur area of India adorn camels with painted decoration, above left, as part of an annual festival. Though the artists decorate in part to attract buyers for their camels, their primary purpose is one of sheer delight and celebration. You might consider installations of Christmas lights, bottom right, and even sculptural hairstyles, top right, as Western cultural equivalents.

DAVE BURMASTER, 2002.
Christmas light display in
Golden Valley, MN.
Photo by Dana Burmaster.

DANA IRWIN,
Pyramids at Giza,
1979. Black and
white photograph.

ED WHEELER, *Formal Garden,* 2002.
Color photograph of a garden in Portugal.
© *Ed Wheeler/CORBIS.*

WILLIAM DAVIS, *(Portrait) David,* 1997.
19 x 17 x 11 inches (48.3 x 43.2 x 27.9 cm).
Stoneware. *Photo by artist.*

CHAPTER 2

THE DESIGN PROCESS

You can go about designing in a variety of ways. Most people tailor their approach to suit the demands of their materials, the requirements of their design purposes, and the temperament and viewpoint they bring to the work. Think of the range of design approaches as existing on a continuum, with most falling somewhere in the middle.

DESIGNING ACCORDING TO A PLAN

One way to approach the design process is to plan everything carefully in advance, often starting with sketches or models, then following them fairly strictly. This tends to work best if you have a specific concept to start with and a clear idea of how you want the finished design to look. From there, you'll lay out a step-by-step plan for executing it.

The Egyptian pyramids, top left, are a magnificent example of designing according to a plan. Considering the extraordinary amount of labor required and the weight of the materials involved, it would have been ludicrous to have attempted

GARY BOLDING,
Cornered Self-Portrait,
2001. 34 x 40 inches
(86.4 x 101.6 cm).
Oil on linen.
Collection of Arthur Goldberg.

these architectural and engineering marvels without a well-developed plan—and a brilliant one at that.

Sometimes, a design's materials require an advance plan. When William Davis set out to document his subject's appearance by sculpting it in stone in *David*, facing page, right, he definitely needed a plan. Once stone is chipped away, there's no getting it back.

Another reason an artist might work according to a plan is to save time and heartbreak in the long run. Gary Bolding, for example, uses an especially labor-intensive painting technique. So, before he painted *Cornered Self-Portrait*, above, he worked out exactly what he wanted the design to say and how he wanted it to look. The alternative would have been painstaking painting and repainting to position the detailed head exactly where he wanted it.

Finally, traditional formal garden designs, facing page, bottom left, are wonderful examples of carefully calculated orchestrations of shape, color, texture, form, and linear movement.

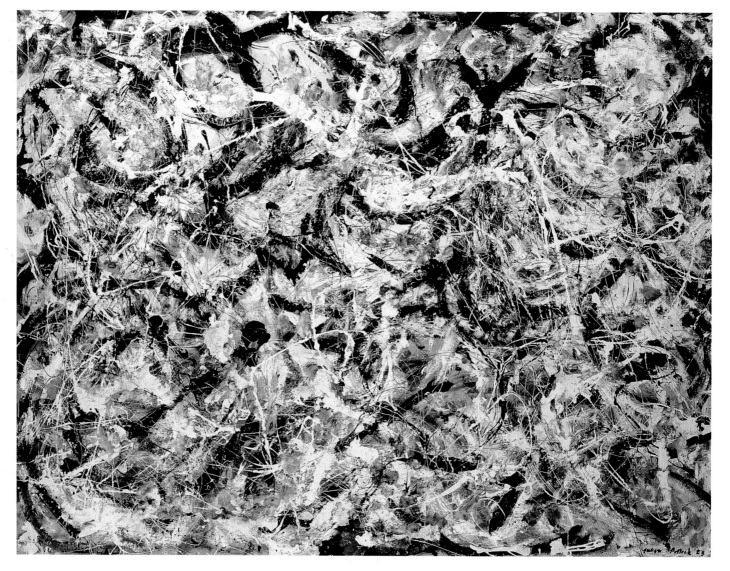

JACKSON POLLOCK,
Greyed Rainbow, 1953.
72 x 96⅛ inches
(182.9 x 244.2 cm).
Oil on canvas.
*Reproduction, The Art
Institute of Chicago,
Chicago, IL (Gift of the
Society for Contemporary
American Art, accession
number 1955.494).*

DESIGNING BY ACTING AND RESPONDING

Another way to design is to decide it isn't always necessary, desirable, or even possible to be in control of a design process. Instead, you might want to put some visual elements in a *design space*, then let the design evolve as you move them around, introduce new elements, veil some, remove others, and continue to respond until you feel the process is complete.

In the fine arts, this approach is a uniquely 20th-century phenomenon, recognized first in the works of Abstract Expressionist artists. Jackson Pollock is one of the most well known; his *Greyed Rainbow*, above, is an exciting example of *acting and responding*. A series of drips and streaks of house paint thrown from a stick energize the surface. When he worked, Pollock stood above the unstretched canvas, acting and responding in an intuitive way as he applied more and more paint to the surface. Pollock's unplanned, experimental approach influenced the way many designers and artists now think and work.

While this process of acting and responding is considered a relatively new concept in the fine arts, it's not new at all to many craftspeople. Makers of what are known as "crazy quilts," like *Evening Star Sampler* by Ena Marie Flynn,

ENA MARIE FLYNN, *Evening Star Sampler,* 1997-1999.
54 x 64 inches (135 x 160 cm). Cotton, silk, satin, velvet, brocade fabrics, charms, buttons, and beads; embroidered, beaded, appliquéd, hand and machine stitched. *Photo by artist. In the collection of the artist.*

CYNTHIA GILLOOLY, 2002. Flower arrangement; silk calla lillies and silk grass in crystal vase. *Art directed by Susan McBride. Photo by keithwright.com.*

above left, often work on small pieces at a time, using fragments of fabric as they become available. By either adding one piece to the next or by making parts separately and then assembling them into a finished design, these quilters introduce elements and respond over and over until the design is complete.

Actually, we all experiment with this kind of design process in our everyday lives anytime we do something as ordinary as hang pictures, assemble a centerpiece in the middle of a table, or arrange flowers, as Cynthia Gillooly did with silk calla lillies and silk grass in a crystal vase, above right.

LAURA ELIZABETH GREEN, *Swimming Suits,* 1986.
4 x 3 feet x ½ inch (1.2 x .9 m x 1.3 cm). Appliqué, trapunto, quilting, mixed media, swimsuit fabric, plastic fish. *Photo by Mike Laurance.*

THE MIDDLE GROUND

Rather than situate themselves firmly at one end of the spectrum, most designers combine aspects of both approaches, and work somewhere in the middle.

Laura Elizabeth Green combines the two design approaches beautifully in *Swimming Suits*, left. She arranges the major visual element—the repeated swimsuit shape—into a planned and orderly grid. The swimsuit motif repeats in nearly identical scale, which enabled her to then compose more by acting and responding, arranging and rearranging the swimsuit forms until the design fell into place.

Painters who work *plein air* (outdoors) and *alla prima* (all at once, set in wet), may start with a plan, but they naturally incorporate acting and responding into their approach. Sandra D. Lloyd did so in *Monhegan Island #12*, facing page, top. She set out a rough design structure to begin with. Then, standing on the cliffs of Monhegan Island, Maine, she did more than simply attempt to describe what she saw at a single moment in time. As she worked, clouds moved, light changed, and shadows shifted. Lloyd embraced aspects of one moment, incorporated elements that occurred later, shifted some around, took some out, and altered others until her composition fell into place. The result was an edited, altered, and distilled composite of her experiences over time—and of her original plan.

The stone wall documented in Thomas Rain Crowe's photograph, facing page, bottom, was clearly built through a combination of structured planning and acting and responding. Its location was likely planned for purposes of sectioning off the terrain and containing farm animals. The stones themselves, gathered on site, were probably chosen specifically for their long, thin shape and unity of color and texture. And the builders of the fence chose to place most of those stones in the same vertical orientation.

Nonetheless, a great deal of improvisation and chance occurrence went into the wall's construction. The exact tilt of each stone, for example, was determined primarily by how it fit with others, and the interesting patterns formed by the empty spaces in between were the serendipitous result.

SANDRA D. LLOYD, *Monhegan #12,*
2001. 5 x 7 inches (12.7 x 17.8 cm).
Oil on clay board. *Photo by Beach Photo
and Video.*

THOMAS RAIN CROWE,
Irish Wall, 1995.
Color photograph.

CHAPTER 3

VISUAL ELEMENTS

Think of visual elements as the raw materials you use in design. As you select and position them in a design space, they join with others to form a group or community of elements that relate to one another. These relationships create your finished design. Visual elements fall roughly into five categories: line, mark, texture, shape or form, and color. This chapter introduces you to all of them.

CY TWOMBLY, *Untitled (White Roma),* 1958. 52 x 62 inches (132.1 x 157.5 cm). Oil, crayon, pencil on canvas. *Collection of David Geffen, Los Angeles, CA.*

LINE

A line is the recorded movement of a dot on its journey from one point to another. The length of a line is much greater than its width, but beyond that, the qualities of lines vary greatly. They can be long or short, straight or curved, rounded or angular, heavy or thin (see figure 1). Lines also relate to one another in a number of ways. They can run parallel to one another or in a convergent pattern; they can intersect or overlap (see figure 2).

Lines can function in a variety of ways in design.

LINE AS SHAPE MAKER

Whenever a line ventures out on a journey through space and crosses back over itself, it encloses an area. The enclosed area reads as a shape (see figure 3). This sort of linear activity is something like a cowboy's lasso. When the rope or linear element is thrown, the loop at the end can enclose and form a great variety of shapes before settling on a final one.

A line doesn't have to cross over itself to make a shape. It can simply meet or butt up against itself, or, it can imply that it will meet itself to indicate a shape. Also, a line can cross over or meet another line, and the two together can form a shape (see figure 4).

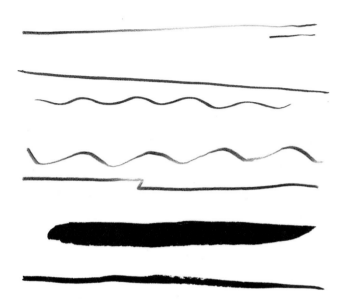

Figure 1

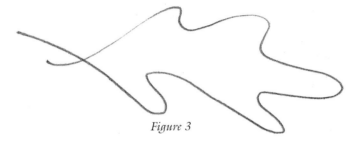

Figure 3

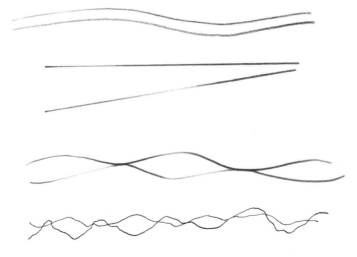

Figure 2

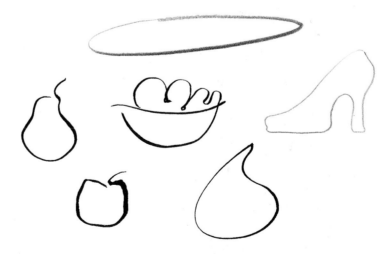

Figure 4

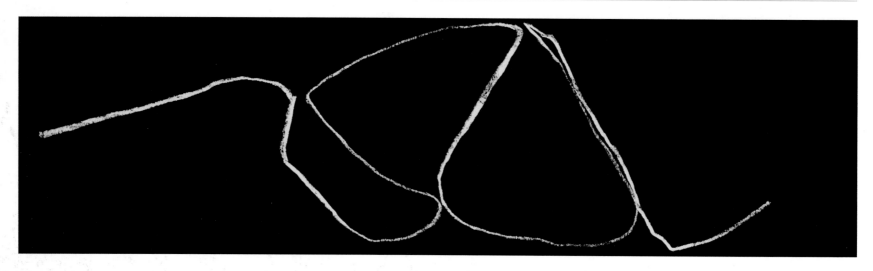

BENEDIKTE AND JAN GROTH, *Sign II,* 1967. 55 x 197 inches (140 x 500 cm). White and black wool tapestry. *Photo by Erling Mandelmann. Collection of Museum of Art, Carnegie Institute, Pittsburgh, PA.*

Benedikte and Jan Groth's tapestry *Sign II*, above, is a wonderful illustration of a range of things line can do and, in particular, the ways line can create shapes. In the center of the composition is a cluster of three shapes formed in various ways.

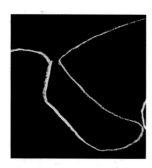

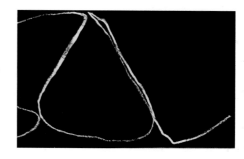

The thin oval to the left is formed by an elongated diagonal movement, from upper left to lower right, which then curves and reverses itself, moving on a diagonal from lower right to upper left.

The modified triangle shape in the center begins with the last movement that formed the thin oval.

A pear-like shape at the right of the cluster begins where the line forms the third side of the triangle.

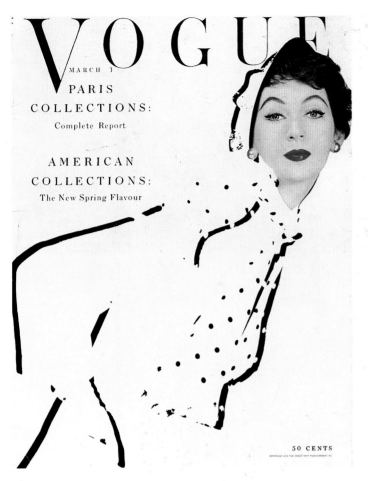

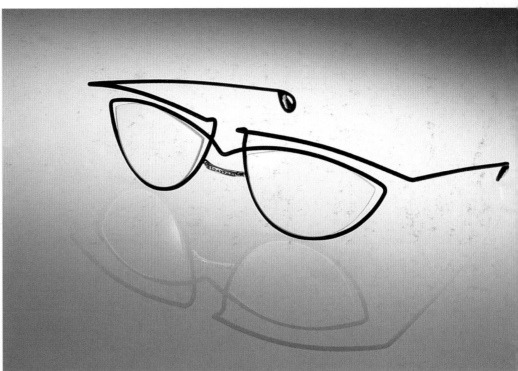

Even broken or lost and found lines can serve most effectively to establish shape. Notice how these kinds of elements establish the shape of the woman's figure in *Vogue's* magazine-cover illustration, above left.

In Debra Stoner's eyeglasses, above right, notice how space is lassoed by line to form the two modified oval shapes that hold the lenses, a tiny shape that forms the bridge of the glasses, and small loops at the end of each side piece of the frame.

Linear movements can create *three-dimensional* form as well. Repeated looping movements in bamboo establish the volume of the covered walkway in Adam and Sue Turtle's photo of the arch at Prafance Gardens, France, bottom right.

ERWIN BLUMENFELD, 1953.
10 x 12 inches
(25.4 x 30.5 cm).
Photograph combined with illustration for March, 1953 *Vogue* magazine cover.
Copyright © 1953 Conde Nast Publications Inc. Reprinted by permission. All rights reserved.

DEBRA STONER,
Judy's Inheritance, 1994.
5 x 5 x 1½ inches
(12.7 x 12.7 x 3.8 cm).
Eyeglasses of steel, platinum, diamonds, lenses; fabricated.
Photo by Marcus Swanson.

ADAM AND SUE TURTLE,
Untitled (arch at Prafance Gardens, France), 1999.
Color photograph of bamboo installation. *Copyright Temperate Bamboo Quarterly, used with special permission.*

Figure 5

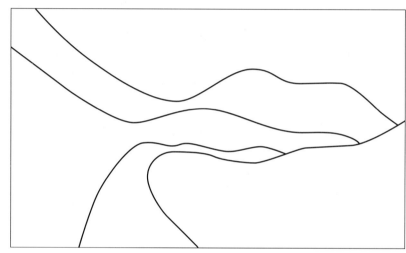

Figure 6

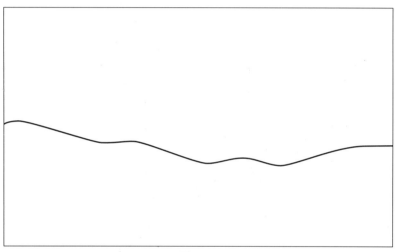

Figure 7

Figure 8

LINE REPRESENTING EDGE

An edge is the place where one shape butts up against another; a line can represent this edge. Figures 5 and 6 show several adjacent shapes of color. Figures 7 and 8 show how their edges translate into line.

John Storrs uses line this way in *Woman with Hand on Chin*, facing page, left. Virtually every line is a symbol for the edge where one shape stops and an adjacent one begins. The line that represents the edge of the shoulder and upper arm on the left, for example, wouldn't exist in real life. Here, it indicates where the shoulder and arm butt up against a shape of color to the left and behind.

Kate Esplen's *Horse Angel*, facing page, right, shows line at work in a similar way in a shallow, three-dimensional space. Almost every bend in Esplen's sculptural wire piece represents the change in the outside edges of the form, such as the contour of the hindquarters or neck.

JOHN STORRS, *Woman with Hand on Chin,* 1931.
12¾ x 8 inches (33 x 20.3 cm). Silverpoint on paper.
The Arkansas Arts Center, Little Rock, AR (Foundation Collection,
purchased with gallery contributions, 1985).

KATE ESPLEN, *Horse Angel,* 2002. 8 x 9 x 2½ inches
(20.3 x 22.9 x 6.4 cm). Aluminum wire. *Photo by Juergen Rust.*

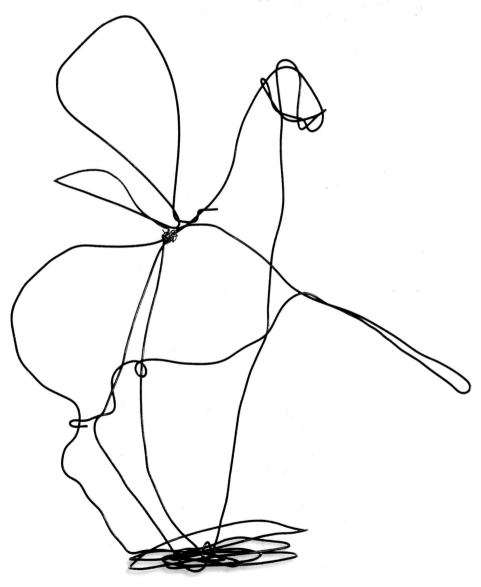

Fence near Cooperstown, NY, c. 1960s. Chestnut split rail. *Photo by Lawrence Hamilton.*

MARY ELLEN LONG, *Rock Spiral,* 1991. 10 feet (3.1 m) in diameter. Outdoor installation of stones in San Juan Mountains, CO. *Photo by artist.*

LINE AS DIRECTION OR MOVEMENT

Another powerful thing that line can do is establish a feeling of direction or motion. You experience this phenomenon when you notice the linearity of a traditional wooden fence as it meanders its way through a field, as the one does in the photograph by Lawrence Hamilton, above. You also see this principle clearly in Mary Ellen Long's *Rock Spiral*, left, where a series of stones is arranged in a linear sequence that spirals in and out from a center point. In Margaret Dahm's *Verdigris Fish Mobile*, facing page, top right, a wire zigzags its way to connect a triangular shape on the left with a semicircle on the right.

In former Denver Bronco Steve Foley's football play diagram, facing page, bottom, line is used to indicate a variety of directional movements to be taken by eleven players in unison to gain yardage. You use line in this same kind of schematic manner anytime you sketch a map to show someone how to get to your home, workplace, or favorite restaurant.

Michael Sherrill's ceramic sculpture *The Garden*, facing page, top left, provides another good illustration of line leading us on directional journeys through space. Sherrill has assembled

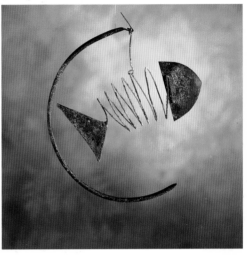

MICHAEL SHERRILL,
The Garden, 1995.
7 feet x 49 inches x 2 feet 6 inches
(2.1 x 1.3 x .7 m). White stoneware,
berium glaze; extruded and pulled,
wheel thrown and altered.
Photo by Tim Barnwell.

MARGARET DAHM,
Verdigris Fish Mobile, 2000.
9 x 9 x 2 inches (22.9 x 22.9 x 5 cm). Copper.
Photo by Sandra Stambaugh.

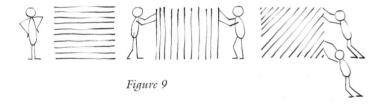

Figure 9

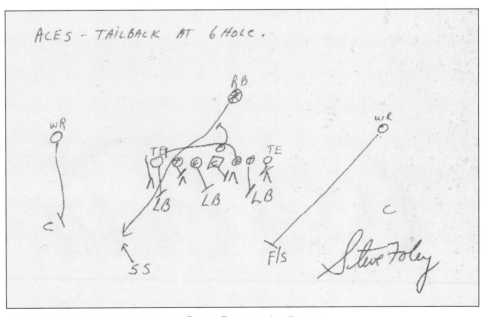

STEVE FOLEY, former defensive back, Denver Broncos, play diagram.

a series of forms that wiggle and gesture. The linear nature of the design is emphasized by the peaks in the forms facing out in this photograph.

Most often, lines indicate movement in one of three ways: horizontally, vertically, or diagonally. If any one of these orientations dominates a design, a particular feeling is established. A design dominated by horizontals, for example, creates a feeling of tranquility and repose. One dominated by verticals is more dynamic, because it runs perpendicular to the floor of gravity. A composition dominated by diagonals is filled with tension, because this movement offers neither the comfort of the horizon nor the sense of intersecting with it. Instead, diagonals tilt, press, and lean in dynamic opposition to both the horizontal and vertical (see figure 9).

PHILIP EVERGOOD,
Profile of a Young Boy,
c. 1930. 12½ x 8⅞ inches
(31.8 x 22.5 cm).
Ink, pencil, conte
crayon on paper.
*The Arkansas Arts Center,
Little Rock, AR (Foundation
Collection, 1977).*

FRANK ROBINSON, c. late 19th century. Product logo. *Registered trademark of The Coca-Cola Company.*

LINE FOR EMPHASIS

Changes in line quality can create areas of emphasis in a design. In *Profile of a Young Boy*, left, Philip Evergood purposely changes the *weight* of the line to establish a hierarchy of emphasis. The lines that represent the front contours of the boy's face are heavier than almost all other lines in the design. Because of this, our attention is drawn to this area first. The lines that form the eye are similarly emphasized; so are a couple of notes at the back of the head. The lines representing the back of the neck and the ear are medium in weight, catching the eye next. Finally, contour lines that indicate the boy's shoulder and arm have enough weight to activate the bottom of the space, and a solitary note at the wrist is just strong enough to place a bit of emphasis in the lower left.

LINE AS RHYTHM

Visual rhythm is analogous to musical rhythm; each is experienced as a series of beats. Look no further than your own signature—or a familiar logo, bottom left—to get an idea of what rhythm is and how line can establish it. The linear and looping movements in the Coca-Cola symbol repeat in a simple, orderly, elegant rhythm. The angles of the characters repeat the same right-leaning tilt, with some of the notes larger or more emphatic than the rest.

LINE AS SYMBOL

Sometimes, line can be used purely as symbol. Look at the numeral "3" on the opening page of this chapter, page 32, or at the three variations on the facing page. The line that symbolizes it forms a double looping movement, which is closed on the right side and open on the left.

LINE TO CREATE DEPTH

Line alone can create a feeling of depth in a space. In *two-dimensional* design, this involves creating the illusion of three dimensions. Willem de Kooning changes the quality of line, along with contrasts of color, to create depth in *Untitled*, facing page, right. He varies the thickness and thinness of the linear elements to alternately push forward and recede. Not only are some lines thicker than others, but sometimes the same line varies in its thickness as it meanders through space.

WILLEM DE KOONING, *Untitled,* 1984. 88 x 77 inches (223.5 x 195.5 cm). Oil on canvas. *Courtesy Thomas Ammann Fine Art, Zurich, Switzerland.*

In drawing, a line that varies is known as a *weighted line*. The thicker lines advance to the front, while lines of medium weight fall back by contrast. Thin and very thin lines seem to recede further still, all creating an effective feeling of depth.

LINE AS VALUE BUILDER

Value is the relative degree of lightness and darkness of an area or shape. A series of lines acting together can establish it with density. Figure 10 shows a series of identical shapes containing parallel horizontal lines, or *hatching*. As the lines appear closer together, the space becomes more dense, and the value is darker. Figure 11 shows the same idea at work, only this time the repeated parallel horizontal lines are accompanied by repeated parallel vertical lines that cross over the horizontals, *crosshatching*. Finally, figure 12 shows another way lines can be configured to establish value: *contour crosshatching*.

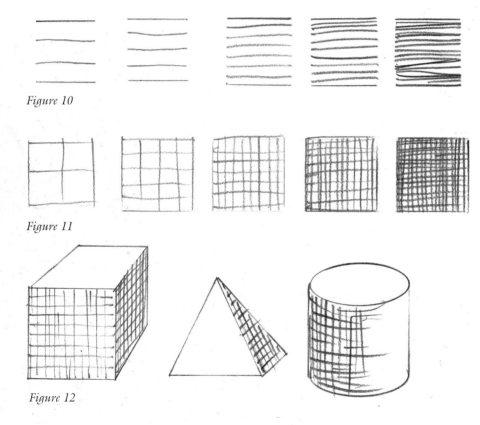

Figure 10

Figure 11

Figure 12

PABLO PICASSO, *Head of a Young Man,* 1923. 24½ x 18½ inches (62.1 x 47.4 cm). Grease crayon. *Courtesy of Brooklyn Museum of Art, Brooklyn, NY.*

Pablo Picasso's grease crayon drawing *Head of a Young Man*, above right, is a great example of using line to build value. In this wonderfully delicate rendering of a head lit strongly from one side, Picasso varies the density of the hatched line to produce a full array of value. Almost all the lines in the drawing are engaged in contour crosshatching. This is most evident in the neck, where the dominant set of lines curves in a parallel fashion, echoing the cone-like neck, while a few light vertical hatches echo the sides of the form.

Lines create value in our experience of architectural forms, too. In John Roebling's *The Brooklyn Bridge*, facing page, top, photographed from above, the suspension cables are brightly lit to read as a series of light lines in space. Sets of these lines, suspended on angles from the tower, create variation in density and are crosshatched by vertical lines running from the road up to the sloping primary cables at the top.

JOHN AUGUSTUS ROEBLING,
The Brooklyn Bridge, 1869-1883.
Suspension bridge. *Photo 1982 by Jet Lowe.*
Courtesy of the Library of Congress.

DOROTHEA LANGE, 1939. Black and white
photograph of a fence built in 1890 in Gem
County, ID. *Courtesy of The Library of Congress.*

LINDA MCNALLY, *Polly Gayton,* 2000.
8 x 10 inches (20.3 x 25.4 cm). Linen
cross-stitch. *Photo by Matthew Thompson.*

In this view, one set of crosshatched lines overlaps a second
set, which overlaps still a third set. The result is a varied
range of values, all of which appear as light in front of the
dark of the river.

Notice a similar phenomenon at work in the lines of the Idaho
fence photographed by Dorothea Lange, above. Sets of parallel logs create crosshatches as we look through one set
and see another. The values here stand as both extreme
lights and darks in relation to the surrounding grasses.
Consider Linda McNally's *Polly Gayton*, right, as well. McNally
uses cross-stitching just as Picasso uses crosshatching: to
build and establish value.

WILLIAM BAILEY, *Seated Nude,* 1978. 15 x 11 inches (38.1 x 28 cm). Pencil on paper. *The Arkansas Arts Center, Little Rock, AR (Foundation Purchase: Barrett Hamilton Acquisition Fund, 1981).*

EGON SCHIELE, *Arthur Roessler Standing with Arms Akimbo,* between 1912 and 1918. Black chalk. *Courtesy of Albertina Museum, Vienna, Austria.*

LINE TO ESTABLISH MOOD

Figure 13, facing page, shows a range of the expressive qualities line can convey. Take out a piece of paper and try a few yourself. Communities of lines can relate to one another in ways that establish mood as well. Compare the two line drawings above to see how. Both are drawings of human figures, and both consist primarily of black lines on a white surface. Yet, they make radically different emotional statements.

LINE AS SUBJECT

There's one case in which line is not an *abstraction*. That's when, instead of symbolizing something else, line itself functions as the subject of a design. Cy Twombly's *Untitled (White Roma)*, page 32, is a prime example. It consists of nothing but line's range of expressive qualities and the overall mood evoked by their arrangement. Visually, the design of The Bamboo-Smiths's woven bamboo partition, bottom right, is also all about line, its crisscross patterns, and the shapes and movements it creates. Finally, consider *Muses (Hydra Variation)* by Brice Marden, top right. Again, line, with its overlapping looping movements—along with supporting elements of color— is the entire subject of the design.

Angry/serene

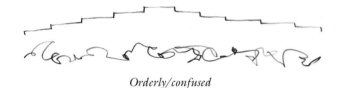

Orderly/confused

Busy/quiet

Rhythmic/lyrical

Figure 13

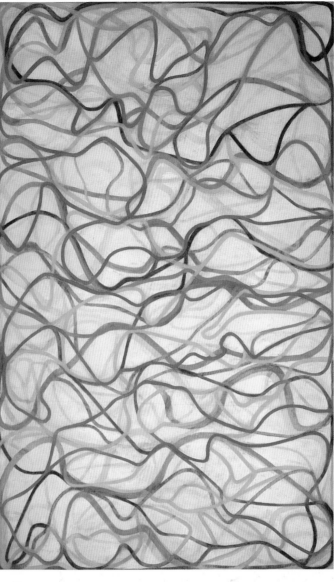

BRICE MARDEN,
Muses (Hydra Version),
1991-1997. 83 x 135 inches (210.8 x 342.9 cm). Oil on linen. *Courtesy Matthew Marks Gallery, New York, NY.*

THE BAMBOO-SMITHS,
Detail of a split and woven bamboo fence panel. Design and photo by The Bamboo-Smiths. Used with permission.

MARK

A mark is the visible impression left on a surface when it's touched by a tool or other object. Designs that feature impressions made by handheld tools, such as brushes, pencils, or etching needles, are often described as showing the "artist's hand." But there are no limits to the range of tools that can be used to make marks. Your elbow, a comb, and a piece of string are all possibilities, and mark-making activities can include everything from burning and sanding to tearing and hole punching. A mark can take on almost any form (see figure 14).

Figure 15

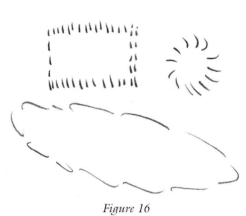

Figure 16

Figure 14

Mark is often seen as just a variation of line. It's true, a series of marks can do many of the things a line can do. They can form implied lines (see figure 15), create shape (see figure 16), establish emphasis (see figure 17), create depth (see figure 18), and so on. But the primary purpose of a mark is to activate a space. In addition, mark can do a number of things in a way that's distinctly different from or has certain advantages over line.

Figure 17

Figure 18

MARK AS ACTION

In most cases, a design begins with an empty space. As soon as there's a mark on the surface, relationships begin and tensions occur. There's contrast between active and passive, textured and smooth, busy and quiet. Many designers use mark in this way to create a quilted pattern in a space. This pattern can even serve as a main organizing principle of the design.

Vincent van Gogh was a masterful mark maker. Take a look at how he uses mark in *Montmajour,* facing page, top.

VINCENT VAN GOGH,
Montmajour,
late 19th century.
19 1/8 x 23 1/4 inches
(48.5 x 59 cm).
Reed pen and ink.
Rijkmuseum, Amsterdam,
Holland.

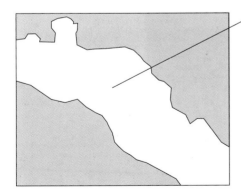

The primary forms and movements are clustered together in a broad diagonal band running from the bottom right, where rock forms appear to go off the edge of the design, to the upper left.

Within this central band is a quilted pattern of busy/quiet.

The remaining spaces in the design form two large triangular areas, one in the upper right, the other in the lower left.

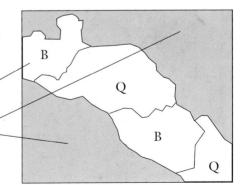

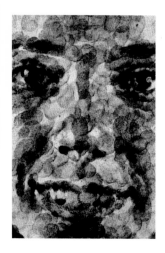

CHUCK CLOSE,
Georgia/Fingerprint I,
1985. 33½ x 27½ inches
(85.1 x 69.9 cm).
Gravure print from
Mylar drawing on paper.
*Collection of the Tampa Museum
of Art, Tampa, FL (Gift of Mr. and
Mrs. Stephen Reynolds,
accession number 1986.201).*

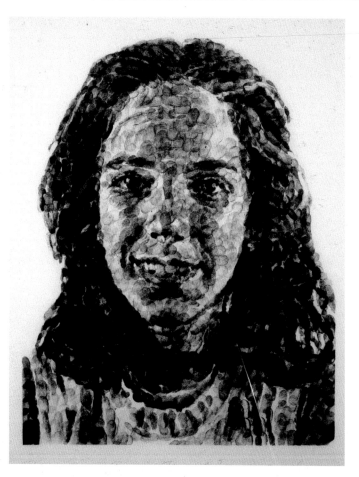

KATHERINE COLWELL,
Juniper, 1996-98.
2⅜ x 2½ inches (6 x 6.4 cm).
Silk and cotton sewing thread
embroidered on linen; straight,
stem, back, and satin stitches.
Photo by artist.

Elizabeth Ryland Mears uses mark to create active/passive contrast in her glass composition *Leaf Series: Goblet with Blue and Green Leaves*, facing page, top left. The surface of the central cup is very smooth and untextured. It derives its weight from its scale and color, a pure, solid, dark blue, with no deviations or variations; nice and quiet. The active and varied series of marks on the bottom give that portion its oomph. The intricate cluster of leaf and branch forms are decorated with a series of small dot, dash, and cross marks in blues and greens, bringing the space to life.

MARK AS SHORTHAND SYMBOL

A series of marks that are effectively chosen, generated, and arranged can act as symbols that represent elements in the visible world. Look back at *Montmajour*, page 47; van Gogh starts with a series of short, parallel hatch marks in clusters to represent grasses and a cluster of short dash marks to represent floral forms. A series of tiny horizontal dashes in the architecture near the upper left edge represents building blocks.

MARK AS UNIFIER

Whenever one kind of mark is used exclusively or as the dominant element in an arrangement, it contributes to a feeling of sameness in the space, which can help a design hold together. In Chuck Close's *Georgia/Fingerprint I*, above, amid the strong, dynamic contrasts of light/dark and busy/quiet, the surface is activated with nothing but the artist's fingerprint, giving the design a feeling of clarity and unity. Katherine Colwell's embroidery composition *Juniper*, bottom left, is similarly unified by the overall repetition of short, vertical stitch marks.

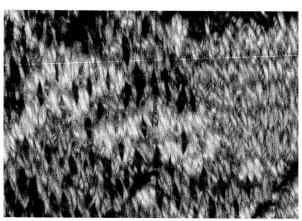

JOANNA GOLLBERG, *Layered Cuff Bracelet,* 2002. 3 x 6½ x 1 inches (7.6 x 16.5 x 2.5 cm). Copper, brass, sterling silver; fabricated, riveted, chased. *Photo by keithwright.com.*

CY TWOMBLY, *Untitled (Roma),* 1961. 100-¾ x 121 inches (256 x 307 cm). Oil paint, oil-based house paint, wax crayon, lead pencil on canvas. *Photo by Jochen Littkemann, Berlin, Germany. Daros Collection, Switzerland.*

ELIZABETH RYLAND MEARS,
Leaf Series: Goblet with Blue and Green Leaves, 1993. 14 x 12 x 4 inches (35.6 x 30.5 x 10.2 cm). Flameworked and assembled glass. *Photo by John Russell.*

MARK AS SUBJECT

As with line, the only time mark is not an abstraction is when it's not symbolizing something else, but serving as the subject of a design. Cy Twombly's *Untitled (Roma),* right, is a great example of a design that uses mark—supported by line and color—as its subject. It features a pattern of contrasting areas of busy/quiet, open/congested. Different kinds of mark also establish varying sensations of texture. Mark itself is the primary subject in Joanna Gollberg's *Layered Cuff Bracelet,* top right, which features an enticing variety of mark as surface embellishment.

TEXTURE

All objects have actual texture. They feel a certain way when touched, from smooth, gritty, slick, crinkled, or ribbed to bumpy, slimy, or fuzzy. In design, the idea of texture expands to include the notion of imaginary texture, which is created when a series of visual elements (line, mark, or shape) is arranged to evoke a sense of touch. The arrangement elicits an imaginary tactile experience.

ACTUAL TEXTURE

The first thing texture can do in design is the most obvious: it can communicate through touch. Actual texture can often be recognized by the eye as well, and it's present in designs that are primarily two dimensional, as well as those that are three dimensional.

BANDHU DUNHAM, *Flying Furbearing Seaweed Goblet,* 1996. 7 x 3 x 3 inches (17.8 x 7.6 x 7.6 cm). Lampworked borosilicate glass. *Photo by Christopher Marchetti.*

As a functional object that's meant to be touched, actual texture plays a prominent role in Bandu Dunham's *Flying Furbearing Seaweed Goblet*, right. His clear glass piece features wonderful variations in surface texture. It's smooth around the middle of the spherical form, wavy and undulating near the top, and exhibits prominent linear protrusions near the bottom of the sphere and on the thick stem. The wavy and pointy elements contrast strongly with the smoothness of the glass. And whether the protrusions are

LYNA FARKAS, *Untitled (interior design with wallpaper),* 2003. *Photo by keithwright.com.*

interpreted as drips of melting ice or as prickly elements guarding the vulnerable glass form, Dunham's textures and their arrangement dominate the design. Interior decorators pay attention to juxtapositions of texture as well. In the photo above left, notice how the smooth surfaces in the horizontal sequence of mats and frames play nicely against the rougher texture of the surrounding wallpaper.

Don Gurewitz's photograph *Granary*, facing page, left, documents a beautiful and rich array of actual texture. The fine organic texture on the wall of the hut harmonizes with the similar though much more pronounced textures in the nearby stones. Both stand in striking contrast to the linear textures in the straw on the hut roof and floor. In Eric Nelsen's ceramic sculpture *Traveler #25*, facing page, right, the textural contrast is created by the smoothness of the ceramic surface against the hard-edged contours of the carved shapes. The shapes vary nicely, but they function as one textural family that speaks strongly to our sense of touch.

DON GUREWITZ, *Granary,* 1999. Color photograph taken in Dogon country, Mali. *Collection of the artist.*

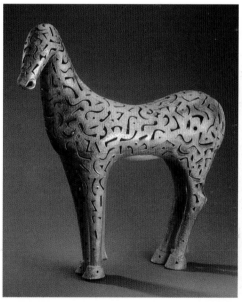

ERIC NELSEN, *Traveler #25,* 1994.
27 x 22 x 10 inches (68.6 x 55.9 x 25.4 cm).
Anagama fired clay; hand built, slab; coiling, thrown, press molded, carved, extruded.
Photo by Roger Schreiber.

ANDY WARHOL,
Unknown Male,
c. 1957. 16³/₄ x 13⁷/₈
(42.5 x 35.2 cm). Black
pen on manila paper.
(insert copyright symbol
here) *The Andy Warhol
Foundation for the Visual
Arts/ARS, NY.*

JANICE PEACOCK,
*Swirl Beads and Zigzag
Vessel Bead,* 1998.
1½ (3.8 cm) and 2 inches
(5 cm) long.
Handmade flameworked
soda-lime glass. *Photo by
artist. Courtesy of the artist.*

IMAGINARY TEXTURE

There's almost no actual texture in Andy Warhol's pencil drawing *Unknown Male,* above left, only the smooth quality of the paper and perhaps some slight impressions from the pressure Warhol used to push down on the pencil as he drew. Instead, Warhol uses line and mark to communicate a strong idea of how the surface of the drawing would feel if touched, from the roughness of his subject's hair and ribbed surface of his sweater to the smoothness of his skin.

Janice Peacock's two glass beads, above right, show the differences and similarities between imaginary texture (right) and actual texture (left).

ACTUAL & IMAGINARY TEXTURE COMBINED

Many designers experiment with combinations of actual and imaginary texture. In the mixed media composition *Nine Golden Pods*, right, Akiko Sugiyama plays a range of actual texture against areas of painted imaginary texture. Compare the little rectangle of crinkled gold leaf to the crinkly feeling of painted passages nearby. Notice, too, the range of texture in the design, from the very slight texture of paint on paper and the nearly smooth round paper discs to the crinkled nature of the gold leaf, the coarseness in the cluster of twigs, and the knobby feeling of the little gold spherical forms attached to the inside of the little door.

Judith Motzkin offers another example in *Trio of Boxes with Woven Windows*, below. The surfaces of these vessels are predominately smooth. In contrast, little window openings cut into each side wall and lid feature coarsely textured woven coil inlay. What makes Motzkin's design exceptionally rich is that these actual textures are mimicked and supported by similar visual textures in the surface decoration of the vessels. Notice in the central vessel, for example, the similarity in textural feeling between the coil inlay and the series of criss-crossing lines on the lid.

AKIKO SUGIYAMA, *Nine Golden Pods,* 2000. 16 x 16 x 6 inches (40.6 x 40.6 x 15.2 cm). Hand-coiled rice paper glued to foam board; 2-ply vellum painted with water pigment and textured; rice paper wrapped around polyester fiber and embellished with gold leaf; twigs, waxed linen, matte medium, glue. *Photo by Laura Parker.*

JUDITH MOTZKIN, *Trio of Boxes with Woven Windows,* 1999. Approx. 10 inches (25.4 cm) tall. Wheel-thrown white earthenware clay, woven coil inlay; burnished with terra sigillata, flame painted with volatilized salts, metals, and combustibles in saggar/pit. *Photo by Bob Barrett.*

ARNOLD ALANEN,
Daisen In: Dry Garden,
1980. Color photograph
taken in Kyoto, Japan;
design attributed to
Kogaku Shuko, 1509.

YVETTE SMALLS,
Ancient Senegalese
Twist, 2002. Hair design.
Model: Kim Simpkins.
Photo by Miyoshi Smith.

KATHERINE MCKEARN
AND DIANE MUSE,
Psycho Moms Bake
a Cake, 1995.
81 x 77 inches
(205.7 x 195.6 cm).
Hand piecing, hand quilting.
Photo by Peter Krumhardt.

TEXTURE AS PATTERN

When texture is established via orderly repetition, the result is a feeling of *pattern*. This dynamic is clear in *Daisen In: Dry Garden*, left. In the tradition of the Japanese Zen garden, this garden floor design is composed of gravel that's raked and sculpted into a soothingly repetitive and orderly configuration. Some of the raked lines run parallel to the garden edge, creating a pattern of straight lines. Others respond to the two cone-like mounds, curving around them. Notice how similar patterning dominates and unifies the arrangement of braided hair, below left.

In the quilt *Psycho Moms Bake a Cake*, below right, Katherine McKearn and Diane Muse use many different textures to produce a stunning variety of pattern. Each piece of fabric has an actual texture of its own. Playing a much more prominent role, however, are the imaginary textures. Pretend you can run your hand over the surface, and imagine the different sensations of touch. Where the pattern is very uniform and repetitious, you'd likely experience a sense of relative smoothness. Where there are large, hard-edged red shapes on white, the pattern is irregular at best, and it would probably feel very bumpy. Travel across to the standing mom's apron, and the pattern feels like a delightful series of little raised spots.

TEXTURE AS WEIGHT AND EMPHASIS

Generally speaking, the more active and frenetic the texture, the more visual weight and the greater emphasis it gives a design space.

Carol Lee Shanks's art-to-wear composition *Copper Tunic*, right, illustrates this point nicely. The majority of this design, made of copper wire and handspun fabric, features woven horizontal and vertical patterns that contain very subtle and graceful undulations. These passages are relatively passive and smooth. In contrast, the large collar is very loosely patterned, full of circular movement, and coarsely textured. It has a feeling of great visual weight and demands the most attention in the arrangement.

Lana Wilson's *Ritual Teapot*, below left, works much the same way. Most of its surface texture consists of orderly patterns of parallel linear movements. The exceptions are the more highly activated surfaces in the upper sections of the legs. Here, the range of texture expands greatly. Impressed lines get broader, large shapes that form faces and hands appear, and little stamped checkerboard and dot patterns emerge. The results are passages of much greater textural variety, tension, and weight.

CAROL LEE SHANKS AND KATHRYN ALEXANDER, *Copper Tunic,* 1997. Collaboration; cloth woven of recycled copper wire and handspun fiber by Kathryn Alexander; garment designed and made by Carol Lee Shanks. *Photo by Don Tuttle.*

LANA WILSON, *Ritual Teapot,* 2000. 14 x 17 x 5 inches (35.6 x 43.2 x 12.7 cm). Stoneware. *Photo by artist.*

CAROLYN LAND, *Entrenched Meanders,* 2001. 20 x 30 inches (50.8 x 76.2 cm). Gesso, paint, burnishing on crescent board. *Photo by artist.*

TEXTURE AS SUBJECT

Finally, just as with line and mark, texture can be elevated to subject-matter status. Carolyn Land's *Entrenched Meanders*, below right, is jam packed with actual textures in shallow relief. She uses corrugated cardboard, string, and a wide range of commercial papers to build up a very rich surface. The composition centers on contrasts between activity and passivity and on a contrasting variety of texture, both actual and imaginary.

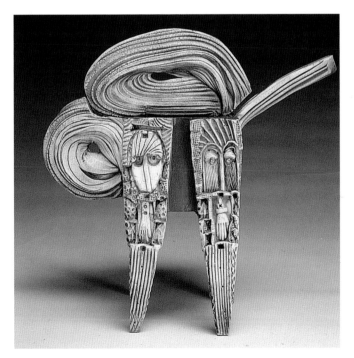

SHAPE AND FORM

Shape is a two-dimensional area with identifiable boundaries. Its dimensions are height and width. There are three primary shapes: circles, squares, and triangles (see figure 19). All other shapes are alterations and combinations of these three. A rectangle, for example, is a square that's extended in one direction. An oval is a circle pulled or stretched in two directions, a "T" is simply one horizontal rectangle stacked on top of a vertical rectangle, and so on (see figure 20).

CHRIS MARTIN,
Winged Bench, 2001.
15 x 43 x 18 inches
(38.1 x 109.2 x 45.7 cm).
Narra, steel.
Photo by George Ensley.

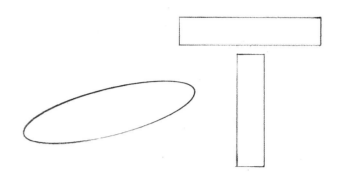

Figure 20

cylinder with a little cone on one end. Most observations about shape can be applied to forms, too.

Shapes come into existence through the establishment of their edges, where one area stops and an adjacent one starts. Edges can be established in numerous ways. They can be either hard (crisp, sharp, fully defined), soft (fuzzy, gentle, implied), or something in between (see figure 22). Many designers use contrasts of hard and soft edge to enrich their arrangements. Consider the airbrushed floral surface decoration on a restaurant-ware coffee cup produced by Sterling China in 1958, facing page, lower left. The stems

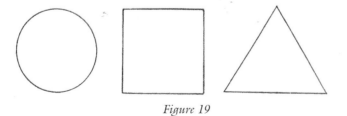

Figure 19

Form is a three-dimensional area with identifiable boundaries. In addition to dimensions of height and width, form exhibits depth. There are five primary forms: cubes, cones, pyramids, cylinders, and spheres (see figure 21). All other forms are alterations, modifications, and combinations of these five. A boxcar on a train, for example, is a cube stretched out in one direction, a sharpened pencil is nothing more than a long

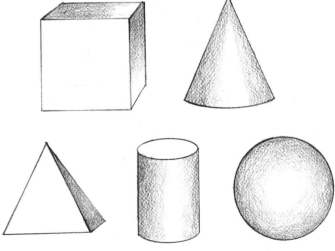

Figure 21

Figure 22

Figure 23

and leaves in green are crisp, clean, and uniformly hard edged. In contrast, the pinkish oval shape that contains the flower is very soft edged, so much so that it's hard to determine exactly where the pink shape stops and the white ground starts.

Shapes can embody a wide range of qualities. They may be large or small, wide or narrow, tall or short (see figure 23). They can also be active or passive (see figure 24), gestural or static (see figure 25), and completely defined or partial and implied (see figure 26).

Figure 24

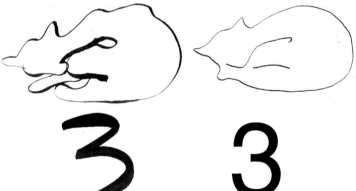

Figure 25

Airbrushed restaurant china cup and saucer, 1958. Commercial vitrified china manufactured by Sterling China. *Photo by Steve Mann. Collection of the author.*

Figure 26

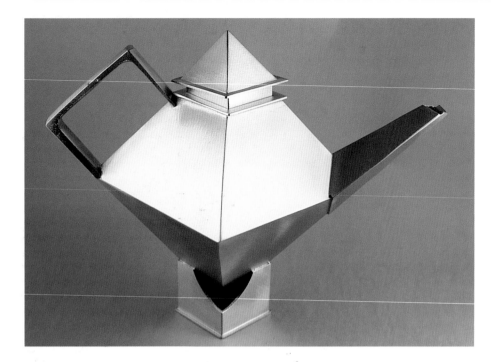

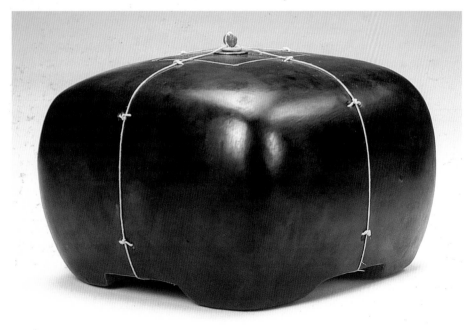

FRED FENSTER, *Teapot,* 1995. 11 x 6 x 5 inches (27.9 x 15.2 x 12.7 cm).
Fabrication using pewter. *Photo by artist.*

SANG PARKINSON-ROBERSON, *Untitled,* 2000. 8 x 8 x 6 inches (20.3 x 20.3 x 15.3 cm).
Pit-fired terra cotta burnished with terra sigilatta; bound with waxed linen; carnelian stone on lid.
Photo by Tim Tew/Studio Tew.

Shapes also fall into two general categories: geometric and organic.

Geometric shapes are those in the square-circle-triangle family. They're characterized by edges that are straight or perfectly curved.

Organic shapes are the opposite. They're based on those found in nature, and are most often rounded and irregular. In contrast to geometrics, organic shapes are each one of a kind. They look as if they've evolved or grown into being.

The two contemporary sculptural forms on the left show the difference.

Fred Fenster's pewter *Teapot*, top, is absolutely geometric. Its main vessel is formed by two pyramids joined at the base, one extending up, the other down. The top is capped off by a flat square, a shallow rectangle, and another flat square. At the pinnacle is another pyramid that serves as the lid. The base is a cube with a circular cutout. Fenster extends the geometry of the design outside the main vessel. The teapot handle forms a rectangle. The spout is an elongated four-sided pyramid. And the space framed by the spout, the top, and an implied line from the top to the tip of the spout is triangular as well.

Sang Parkinson-Roberson's non-functional vessel, bottom, provides a dramatic contrast. Other than the nearly square shape of its lid, this spare and elegant design is completely organic. Though it might be considered vaguely rectangular, every change from top to side, side to side, and side to bottom is soft and indefinite.

Shapes are also either *positive* or *negative*. This distinction involves the relationship of a shape to others and to the space it occupies. When you begin a two-dimensional design with an absolutely empty space, then introduce a shape, the shape is positive. Think of this "positiveness" as the occupation or activation of the space. By definition, a contrasting negative is necessary. The remaining area in the space has shape, too, and is clearly defined by boundaries of its own. This leftover area of space is negative.

John Whipple offers a contemporary look at positive and negative in *Bird in Hand*, facing page. The subject of the painting—a woman holding a bird—is positive. An oval acts as a positive shape containing facial features. Its edges are defined by dark outlines of hair. The massive shape that represents the neck and shoulders in black is positive as well. By contrast, there are two negative shapes in the arrangement, one to the left, the other to the right of the head and neck, above the shoulders. Each of these is a golden amber color.

Even in a design that is as clearly positive-negative as Whipple's, negative shapes can be quite interesting and compelling. Consider the negative shape on the right side of the portrait subject. Its left contour curves, dances, and wiggles in exciting ways, and with as much interest as any other shape in the space. And the shape to the left of the figure is dynamic as well.

Shapes are powerful elements in design. They're also very diverse in function and character. Here are the main ways they operate.

SHAPE AS SHAPE MAKER

Shapes can relate to one another and to the outside edges of the design space in a way that creates additional shapes. In figure 27, for example, the three triangles A, B, and C create all the other triangles. Triangle D occurs as the shape inside or in between A, B, and C. Triangles E, F, G, and H are formed to the outside of A, B, and C. The positive-negative relationship can be interpreted here in several ways. You can see triangles A, B, and C as positives, with the rest as negatives. Or, you can see it the other way around. A third interpretation is to see the entire space as flat, with all the triangles as active figures. In other words, shapes are neither positive nor negative in and of themselves, only in relation to other shapes in a space.

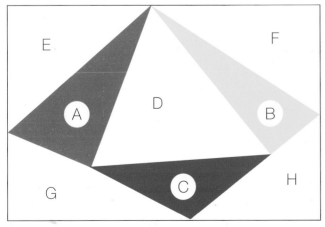

Figure 27

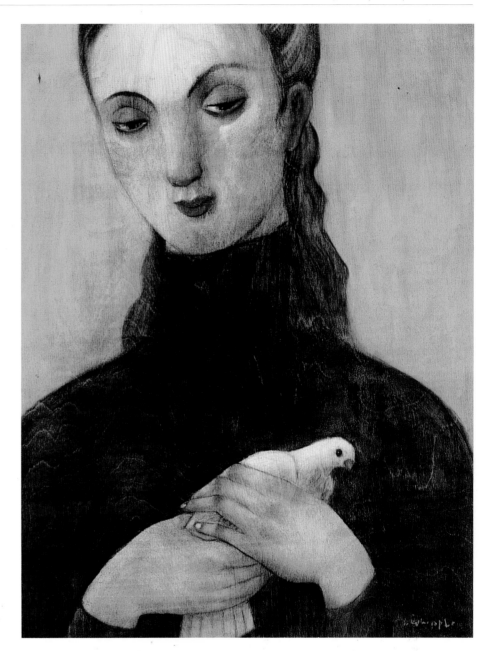

JOHN WHIPPLE, *Bird in Hand,* 2000. 32 x 40 inches (81.3 x 101.6 cm). Charcoal on birch; sealed and coated with layers of translucent oil glazes. *Photo by Randall Smith.*

AL HELD, *Last Series XVII,* 1964-65. 18 x 23⅝ inches (45.7 x 60 cm).
Acrylic on paper mounted on board. ©*Al Held. Courtesy Robert Miller Gallery,
New York, NY.*

JAY RAYMOND, *Lady Dover Model #380,* 1999. Color photograph of iron
manufactured by the Dover Appliance Co., Dover, OH. *Courtesy of Jay Raymond.*

Al Held plays with the idea of shape as shape maker and
with the positive-negative dynamic in his bold composition
Last Series XVII, top left. There are seven shapes in the
space, all geometric, all passive in surface texture, and all
hard edged. Each serves as a container for a single color.
Together, the seven shapes engage the entire space. The
design challenges our assumptions about shape, space, figure, and ground. For example, did the red, blue, dark green,
and dark brown shapes enter the flat rectangular design
space as positive and, in the process, create the complicat-
ed shape of white area left over? It seems so. But consider
the possibility that the long, meandering white shape was
established as positive, resulting in six leftover areas that
were then used to contain red, blue, and black. Or, maybe
parts of the white shape and some of the others were introduced intermittently and improvisationally, with shapes taking
on and giving up positive and negative status along the way,
until the composition came into being.

Jack Mitchell's photograph *Eva Marton, Soprano,* facing
page, is more straightforward. The obvious subject is an
opera singer. But on another level, relationships of shape are
of primary importance in the photographic design. Mitchell's
arrangement consists of one large black shape, the singer's
garment, which reads as positive, and five empty shapes that
read as negative. These six shapes support and frame the
small area of narrative interest: the singer's head, neck, and
the heart-shaped decorative garment trim below the neck.
Look a bit more closely, and notice that the one large positive
shape is composed of a number of smaller ones that are all
modified triangles (see figure 28). The negative shapes are
modified triangles as well (see figure 29).

The vintage steam iron *Lady Dover Model #380,* manufactured by the Dover Appliance Co., bottom left, is another
clear and delightful example of shape making in design.
Notice how one elongated, shiny form serves as the horizontal foundation, while two black resin forms make up the handle. These forms stack up solidly to establish a reverse "C"
movement. The design's real charm is in the negative shape
formed by the three positive ones: the area just above the
base and below the handle top. This shape is completed by
a thin, three-pronged C-shaped movement in silver on the
left, which acts as a counter to the reverse "C" formed by the
blocky, positive masses.

JACK MITCHELL, *Eva Marton, Soprano,* 1985. 11 x 14 inches (27.9 x 35.6 cm). Black and white glossy photograph. © *Jack Mitchell.*

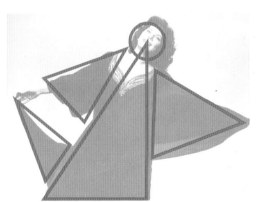

Figure 28

Figure 29

CHRIS SIMONCELLI, *Teapot,*
2001. 11 ½ x 5 x 9 inches
(29.2 x 12.7 x 22.9 cm).
Glazed stoneware.
Photo by artist.

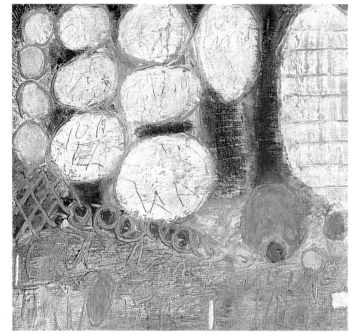

CHARLENE THOMAS,
Back Porch, 2001.
8 x 8 inches
(20.3 x 20.3 cm).
Acrylic on wood.
Photo by Photobition.

**MARTHA MITCHELL AND
RACHEL WARD,**
Compass-Point Mandala,
1996. 17 ¼ x 17 ¼ inches
(43.8 x 43.8 cm).
Stained glass.
Photo by Evan Bracken.

SHAPE AS CONTAINER

Shape can function as a compartment for other visual elements—line, mark, texture, and color—helping keep varieties of surface qualities separate and distinct.

In Chris Simoncelli's *Teapot*, top left, shapes compartmentalize color. Wherever one shape ends and another begins, there's a corresponding change in color.

Similarly, shapes in Charlene Thomas's acrylic painting *Back Porch*, middle left, serve as containers, this time for line, mark, pattern, *and* color. The composition is dominated by ovals. Most contain white, while a few serve as compartments for blue and yellow green. Meanwhile, the largest white oval contains a checkerboard pattern that stops at the edges of the shape. The pattern occurs only one other time, where it's held within the confines of a diamond. The remainder of Thomas's white shapes serve as compartments for calligraphic movements.

Stained glass designs, such as Martha Mitchell and Rachel Ward's *Compass-Point Mandala*, bottom left, are great examples of compartmentalized shapes, created by leading, that serve as containers for color.

There are several less cut-and-dried ways to use shape in design. All have to do with the idea that shapes have *personalities* that assert themselves in an arrangement. Some shapes push while others pull in response. Some speak loudly and assertively; others are quiet and subservient. Some wiggle and dance while others stand elegantly still. One shape can feel as if it's bursting at the seams, and another can seem on the verge of collapse. Shapes can twist, turn, loop, and feel as if they're falling, all depending on their personality. Here are several ways to put this principle to work.

SHAPE AS MOVEMENT AND DIRECTION

If you want a design to be full of movement and tension—the opposite of static and calm—shapes can do the trick all on their own. Movement always flows in the direction of a shape's longest axis. An elongated triangle, for example, indicates movement in the direction of a line running from the middle of its base through its apex. The same is true for other shapes, both geometric and organic (see figure 30). All else being equal, the longer the shape, the stronger the sense of directional movement. Also, shapes with more highly articulated or active edges create movements that are slower, since they take more time to experience (see figure 31). Shapes with no longest axis, such as circles, squares, and equilateral triangles, are the exception. They create no inherent movement.

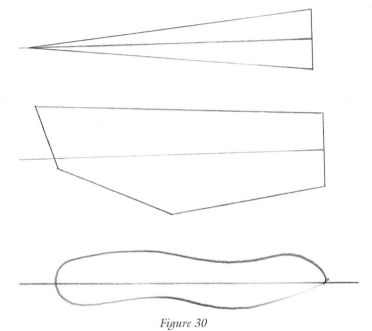

Figure 30

KyungAe Jeon's fiber sculpture *Untitled*, right, provides a crystal-clear example of shape as movement. The singular form leads the eye on an elongated, elegant, looping movement through space. The movement runs along the shape's central axis and, in variations, along its inner and outer contours. The compelling shape of the negative interior space leads the eye on a parallel movement through space, which complements the primary movement.

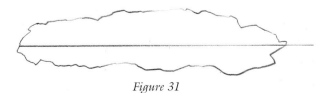

Figure 31

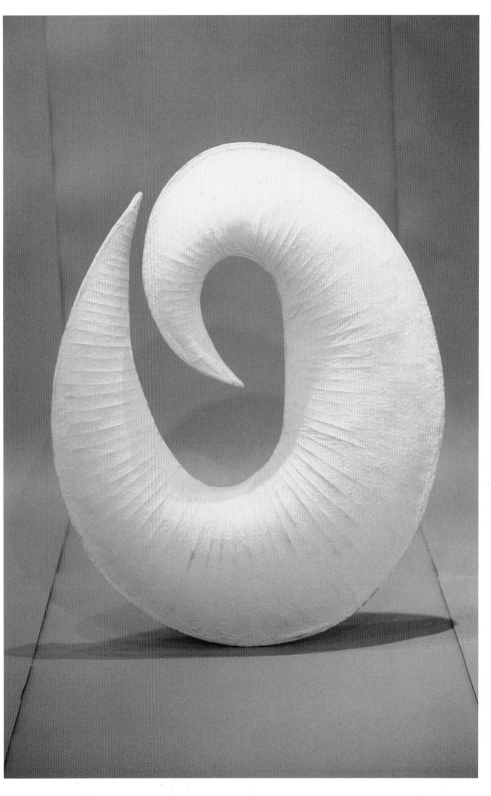

KYUNGAE JEON, *Untitled,* 1998. Approx. 38 x 31 x 8 inches (97 x 79 x 20 cm). Cast and formed handmade flax-hemp paper over armature.

"Lunar Drift"   Renie

RENIE BRESKIN ADAMS,
Lunar Drift, 2000.
6½ x 8⅞ inches
(16.5 x 22.5 cm).
Hand-embroidered cotton.
Photo by artist.
Collection of artist.

LYNN WHIPPLE,
Tulip Series, 1997.
4¼ x 6½ inches
(10.8 x 16.5 cm). Collage;
wax paper, acrylic, charcoal,
pencil, and colored pencil on
wood. *Photo by Randall Smith.*

KIM KELZER, *Desk Lamp,*
1990. 24 x 20 inches
(61 x 50.8 cm).
Cherry wood, copper,
Plexiglas. *Photo by artist.*

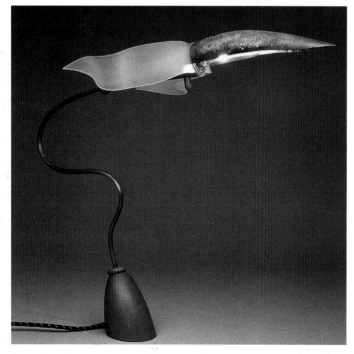

Renie Breskin Adams's *Lunar Drift*, above left, shows how shapes of similar thrust can be arranged to make a powerful, singular directional statement. Each one of the cups, saucers, pitchers, and teapots on the table leans on the same diagonal, from lower left to upper right. They're urging us up and right to the top corner, where a partial crescent moon appears on the horizon. Other shapes support this movement. The two trees and three distant figures form an arcing movement in that direction, which is vaguely echoed by the movement of the banana on the table. Even the movements of the corners of the tablecloth point in a curving fashion to the top and right.

Lynn Whipple's *Tulip Series*, above right, features several shapes with distinct personalities. Each creates movement. The longest, the machete-type shape, loops up and left, wobbles, turns right and broadens, then curves back down a touch. Below it are two modified ovals. The larger indicates a movement up and down. The smaller moves slightly left-right. Finally, the top of the space contains leaf-like shapes that point diagonally. Kim Kelzer's *Desk Lamp*, facing page, bottom, indicates one large directional movement, similar to Whipple's machete shape, this time in three dimensions.

SHAPE AS GESTURE

For an example of shapes with real personality and definite gesture, consider the community of forms in Leslie Bohnenkamp's *Kate's Herd (Iridescent White)*, top right. All 13 members of the cone family lean to the left, creating a powerful overall movement. What makes this composition especially rich is the contrasting character of the individual shapes. Each zigzags its way up, but some softly loop, and others make more abrupt movements. Some feel as if they reach upward more quickly and powerfully, while others end up leaning more to the side. Also, from the vantage point of this photograph, the family members seem to join together into groupings. The three leading the way to the left seem to be separated a bit from the rest, seven or so huddle together in the middle, and a final cluster of three brings up the rear. As a designer, it can be most helpful to experience shapes and forms as personalities that take on roles in communities.

Buildings may not often seem to be made up of organic forms that gesture in space. But in his design of the Guggenheim Museum Bilbao, bottom right, Frank Gehry has arranged just that. Already considered a milestone in contemporary art, the structure is composed of a community of individual forms clustered together. Each is organic, and each twists, turns, or leans. One pushes against the next, another stops that movement and initiates a new one. Some shapes serve as underlying support, while others extend freely into the surrounding space. The end product is an extraordinarily animated structure.

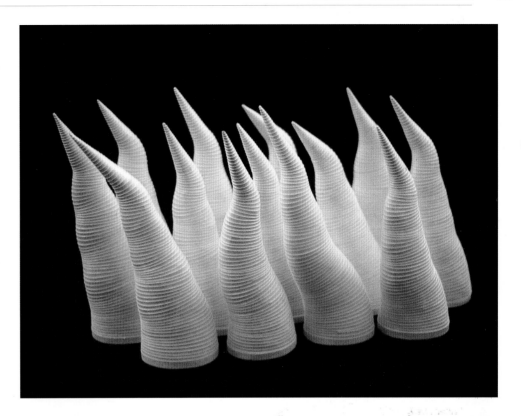

LESLIE BOHNENKAMP, *Kate's Herd (Iridescent White),* c. 1979. Approx. 16½ inches (41.9 cm) tall. Paper sculpture. *Courtesy of Joseph Rickards Gallery, New York, NY.*

FRANK GEHRY, *Guggenheim Museum Bilbao,* 1997. *Photograph by David Heald ©The Solomon R. Guggenheim Foundation, New York, NY.*

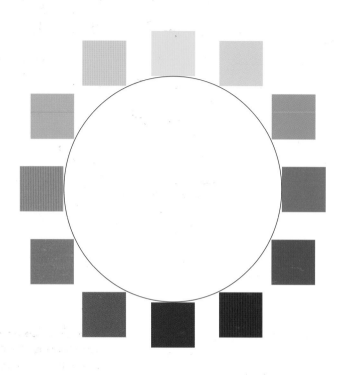

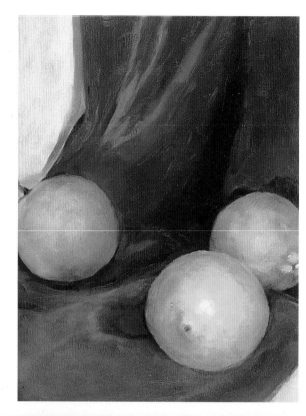

GUS RILEY,
Lemons on Velvet,
1997. 8 x 10 inches
(20.3 x 25.4 cm).
Oil on board.
Photo by Beach Photo.

Figure 32

SUSAN PAPA, *Untitled,* 1998.
9 x 10 x 6 inches
(22.5 x 25 x 15 cm).
Red earthenware; slab built,
extruded, carved, sgraffito,
underglazed, waxed.
Photo by Eric Norbom.

Figure 33

COLOR

Color is probably the most complex visual element. It can function in many ways, and its impact on our experience of the world is profound. This final section of the chapter covers the four main color contrasts and introduces some hands-on challenges to help you experiment with them.

Our experience of color is entirely dependent on light, much like an audible frequency of sound defines what we hear as pitch in music. The surfaces of objects have no color in and of themselves. What we perceive as color is actually rays of light reflected from the object's surface. They give the object its *hue*—what we think of as its redness, blueness, yellowness, and so on. Hues are traditionally organized in relation to each other on a wheel.

A color wheel begins with the most basic colors, called *primary* (see figure 32). Red, yellow, and blue are considered primary colors because they're irreducible, meaning they can't be created by mixing other colors together. Primary colors are located one-third of the way around the wheel from each other. Gus Riley's still-life painting *Lemons on Velvet*, facing page, top, is an example of a composition that gives the primaries center stage.

When you mix any two primaries to create a color exactly halfway between, the color you produce is a *secondary*: orange, green or purple (see figure 33). Secondaries come about in the following combinations: red and yellow make orange, yellow and blue create green, blue and red produce purple. Susan Papa's *Untitled*, facing page, bottom, is an example of a design that uses secondary colors exclusively.

To fill the remaining spaces on the color wheel, you'd mix each abutting primary-secondary color pair to get a color halfway in between. The resulting colors are *tertiary*.

The complete color wheel represents the sequence of colors found in a rainbow. They're the raw color materials you have to work with when designing. Harvey K. Littleton uses them all in *Four Seasons*, above.

Colors located opposite one another on the wheel are referred to as *complements*. Complementary colors enhance and complete each other.

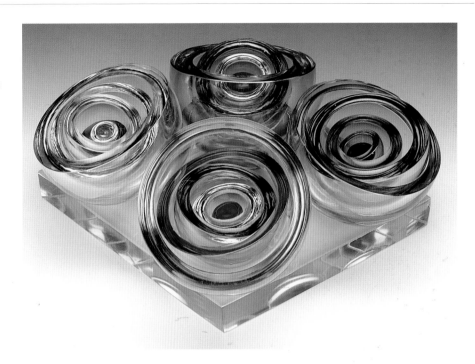

Colors located next to one another on the color wheel are referred to as *adjacents*. Designs that restrict color to contrasting adjacents are naturally unified and harmonious.

Color combinations and juxtapositions can result in contrasts that also create tension and evoke feeling in a design. Here's what color can do:

1. Create a feeling of light and dark (contrast of value).

2. Create a feeling of pure and dull (contrast of *saturation*).

3. Create a feeling of warm and cold (contrast of *temperature*).

4. Create a feeling of completeness (contrast of complements and contrast of complementary pairs).

The next four sections (pages 68-93) explore these uses of color in detail. They also follow the structure you'll find in Chapters 5 through 10; each features an overview, examples, and hands-on exercises.

HARVEY K. LITTLETON, *Four Seasons,* 1977. 5⅜ x 10¼ x 10⅛ inches (13.6 x 26 x 25.7 cm). Blown, cut, and polished potash glass with various coloring oxides. *Gift of Paul and Elmerina Parkman. Smithsonian American Art Museum, Washington, DC/Art Resource, NY.*

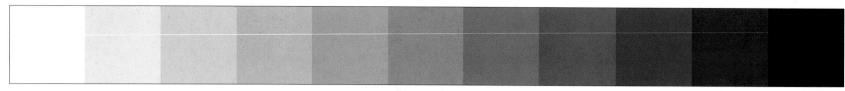

Figure 1

VALUE

CONTRAST OF LIGHT AND DARK

Value is the relative degree of lightness or darkness of a color. The relationship between light and dark in a design is contrast of value. Since every color has a degree of lightness and darkness, you're really working with contrast of value all the time, whether you're aware of it or not.

A design that contains little or no contrast of hue is referred to as *monochromatic*. When you have no contrast of hue, you also have no contrast of saturation, temperature, or any of the other color characteristics we'll discuss in the next sections. In the absence of these contrasts, compositions in monochrome emphasize and heighten the one color contrast that's left: light and dark.

Monochromatic arrangements can consist of any one color, plus variations of that color that occur when it is diluted with white and/or black. Or, they can consist simply of white, black, and the range of grays in between. Black mixed with white in differing amounts creates the broadest possible range of value, so we'll work with that in the examples here.

Figure 1 presents a value scale, a series of eleven squares representing ten equal *intervals* in a movement, white to black. When you design in monochrome, think of this scale as representing the "keyboard" you'll play, with each of the grays making up a part of it. You see monochromatic designs all around you,

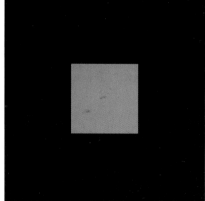

Figure 2

every day. Whenever you see a black-and-white photograph, for example, that's a design in monochrome. A pencil drawing? Yes, indeed. Something printed on a black-and-white laser printer? That too.

As with all relationships of color, keep in mind that light and dark are relative terms. Figure 2 shows two large squares, one black and the other white, each containing a small gray square in the middle. Notice how the gray inside the black appears to be quite light, while the gray inside the white appears much darker and heavier. In reality, the grays are identical; it's the context in which we see them that changes our experience. The only values that can be evaluated on their own are black and white.

Finally, shift your focus from monochrome for a moment, and consider how value contrast plays a part, to some extent, in nearly every design. Every color has a gray that's its equivalent in value. Figure 3 shows pure colors matched with grays of the same degree of lightness and darkness. It's apparent right away that these pure colors have very different value equivalencies. Yellow, for example, is the lightest (there's no such thing as a pure yellow that's dark). Fully saturated blue, on the other hand, is clearly darker and relatively heavy. The remaining colors fall somewhere in between. The moral of the story? You're dealing with relationships of light and dark in polychromatic (multi-colored) designs as well, so keep in mind that this dynamic is always in your design mix.

You can see this dynamic in action in *By the Week*, facing page, an acrylic painting by Katharina Keoughan. The composition is absolutely dominated by light-dark contrast, even though several very intense colors are present. Not only are there white whites and black blacks, but virtually everything in shadow reads as a near black. Notice the cast shadows underneath the roofs, underneath the porch to the left, and on parts of the towel and lawn between the cottages. They all read as darks. The same even holds true for the red porch surfaces and the green roof of the building to the right. A bit of blue on one towel and the green of the lawn in the foreground are the only colors that translate as anything near a middle value.

Figure 3

KATHARINA KEOUGHAN,
By the Week, 2000.
28 x 42 inches
(71.1 x 106.7 cm).
Oil on linen. *Photo by artist.*

Grid 1

Grid 2

Grid 1 is an arrangement of white, black, and a range of grays in between. Because it includes the complete range of the value scale, it's full of contrast, making it very bold and dynamic. The space is full of tension and agitation, and the arrangement evokes a feeling of liveliness.

Grid 2, on the other hand, features grays from the light to light-medium end of the scale. Because of its limited value range, the space feels more united. The tension in the space is not as dramatic; its mood is relatively serene. And because the members of the community are all nearer to white than black on the value scale, the arrangement feels open, light, and airy.

Contrast that to the feeling in Grid 3, where the elements are all quite dark. The mood is relatively quiet here as well, but certainly not light and airy. The space seems very full and relatively dense.

Grid 3

GEORGES SEURAT,
The Sleeper, c. 19th century.
9¾ x 12¼ inches
(24.7 x 31.2 cm).
Pencil drawing. *Photo by Michèle Bellot. Louvre, Paris, France. Réunion des Musées Nationaux/Art Resource, NY.*

Examples

In *The Sleeper*, above, post-Impressionist artist Georges Seurat eliminates all other elements and contrasts; shapes of value tell the whole story. The majority of the space (the shape that makes up the shoulder and torso) is at the light end of the value scale. A significant secondary portion of the design (the figure's hair, hat, and portions of the space behind) is at the dark end. The resulting contrast makes for a clear, strong arrangement. But then, key portions of the space—small in area but featuring primary descriptive elements such as the ear, cheek, eye, nose, and adjoining shoulder—are mainly in the middle range of the value scale. Because these elements belong neither to the very dark nor the very light ends of the scale, they really stand out and become the primary focus.

SYLVIA TAYLOR, *Kitchen Sink at Clandeboye,* 1999. 5½ x 8 inches (14 x 20.3 cm). Linoleum print.

LAURIE SYLWESTER, *Falling Man, Ascending Woman—You Decide,* 1996. 17 x 9 x 9 inches (43.2 x 22.9 x 22.9 cm.). Wheel thrown, glazed, raku fired. *Photo by Ed Doell.*

Ceramist Laurie Sylwester takes value contrast to its limit to create the highly dynamic *Falling Man, Ascending Woman—You Decide*, right. This arrangement features extreme white, distressed white, and absolutely black black. There's nothing in between. Sylvia Taylor's linoleum print *Kitchen Sink at Clandeboye*, above, is dominated by value extremes as well, making for a bold and lively presentation. Notice how both Sylwester's and Taylor's arrangements relate directly to Grid 1, page 70. Conversely, consider how the narrow range of light-middle values in Dan Massey's photograph *From Bala Catamaran Club*, facing page, top right, evokes a feeling of quiet and serenity. His composition relates directly to the arrangement in Grid 2.

Edward Eberle's *Teapot Study*, facing page, top left, is so rhythmically rich and contains so many delightful variations of a circular motif that limiting its palette to monochrome is essential to the clarity of the design. It gives it unity and adds a feeling of stability and even stateliness to an arrangement that's other-wise dynamic, even Baroque. With other color contrasts eliminated from the equation, the one that remains (light and dark) takes center stage. The value contrast establishes patterned and sequential movements that encourage the eye to journey up, down, and around the form in a variety of ways.

Still Life with Letter by Richard Diebenkorn, facing page, bottom, is a superb orchestration of light-dark contrast. Diebenkorn disperses a series of diverse black notes

throughout the space, leading the eye on a satisfying journey. The black wedge of one page of the open book butts up against the white page to draw the eye to the upper right. The bottom right edge of the book points down and left toward the little coffee cup, which casts a powerful dark shadow. Next, a circular shape pulls the eye toward the left, by virtue of its whites and blacks on the gray ground. Finally, the thin, black, horizontal bar on the top edge pulls us up and to the left. Notice, too, how Diebenkorn uses a bit of ochre color to take us from the end of that bar back down on an angle toward the black page again.

EDWARD S. EBERLE, *Teapot Study,* 1992.
10 x 10½ x 5¼ inches (25.4 x 26.7 x 13.3 cm).
Terra sigillata on porcelain. *Photo by artist.*

DAN MASSEY, *From Bala Catamaran Club,* 2001.
Black and white photograph. *Courtesy www.danmassey.co.uk.*

RICHARD DIEBENKORN, *Still Life with Letter,* 1961.
20⅝ x 25⅝ inches (52.4 x 65.1 cm). Oil on canvas.
Collection of the City and County of San Francisco. Photo courtesy of the San Francisco Arts Commission.

Exercises

■ EXERCISE 1

CREATING A VALUE SCALE

Your first hands-on challenge is to create a value scale similar to the one in figure 1, page 68. A bit like practicing scales as a warm-up to playing the piano, this exercise helps familiarize you with the instrument you'll play when you incorporate light-dark contrasts into a design. At the same time, it sharpens your eye.

The value scale is a series of equal steps from light to dark. You want the scale to be similar to a staircase in a house; each step needs to represent an identical interval in the movement from one end to the other. (Think how awkward it would be to walk up a staircase where the first step was 6 inches [15.2 cm], the next a foot and a half [45.7 cm], the next 2 inches [5 cm], and so on.) You also want the surface of each square to be nice and smooth, without contrasting marks and changes in density; those differences would interfere with your ability to judge the flow of the scale.

You don't need to be an experienced artist or craftsperson to do this, nor do you need fancy tools and materials. It can be a bit of a challenge, however, to create a scale with even intervals. You may want to give it a few tries until you come up with a value scale you're satisfied with.

What You Need

Ruler

Pencil

Rectangular surface in white or midtone gray, such as a flat piece of heavyweight paper, cardboard, or mat board, at least 12 x 6 inches (30.5 x 15.2 cm)

White paint (anything from acrylic craft paint to house paint to oil)

Black paint (same media as you selected for the white paint)

Small brush

Mixing tool

Cleaning materials (mineral spirits or turpentine for oil, water for other paints, and a rag)

Palette to mix paint on, such as a plastic lid

What You Do

1. With the ruler and pencil, lightly mark off a horizontal row of nine adjoining squares, each 1 x 1 inch (2.5 x 2.5 cm) (see figure 4). Above each square, number 1 through 9 from left to right.

2. Fill in square number 1 with absolutely solid black.

3. Fill in square number 9 with absolutely solid white.

4. Using a mixture of white and black paint, fill in square 5 with a gray that you judge to be halfway between white and black.

5. Now, fill in square number 3 with a gray you consider to be halfway between black (number 1) and your middle gray (number 5). Fill in square number 7 with a gray you judge to be halfway between white (number 9) and your middle gray.

6. Compare the squares carefully to see if the intervals seem the same. For example, does it seem as if there's a bigger jump between 9 and 7 than between 7 and 5, or vice versa? Make any adjustments you might need by lightening or darkening one or more of the squares.

7. Once you're reasonably satisfied that the intervals are equal, complete the rest of the scale by mixing a gray that's halfway between each of the grays you've got. This will give you the grays for squares 2, 4, 6, and 8.

8. Once again, by isolating groupings of three in a row (you might cover the rest of the squares with pieces of paper), check to see if some of the intervals seem to be bigger or smaller than the rest, and make adjustments. Your goal: nine even steps, like a stairway in a house.

■ EXERCISE 2

COLOR-TO-VALUE TRANSLATIONS

As noted earlier, every color has a gray that's its equivalent in terms of light and dark. Now you'll get some practice making judgments about those equivalencies. You're going to match swatches of color with grays you'll mix to represent the value equivalent of each.

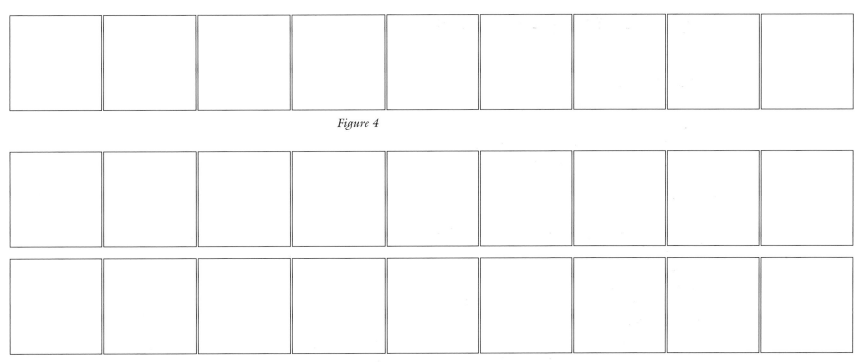

Figure 4

Figure 5

What You Need

Materials used in Exercise 1

Several magazines

Scissors

Adhesive (craft glue, spray adhesive, etc.)

What You Do

1. With the ruler and pencil, lightly mark off two horizontal rows of nine adjoining squares, each 1 x 1 inch (2.5 x 2.5 cm). These two rows should be parallel (see figure 5).

2. Leaf through a magazine or two and pick out some swatches of color, including some primaries and secondaries and some lights, darks, and midtones. Make sure to select a dull color or two, such as a muddy brown or a greenish gray. Make sure, as well, that each swatch is absolutely solid and consistent throughout, with no variation or activity.

3. Cut out 1-inch (2.5 cm) square samples of the colors; you'll need nine altogether.

4. Paste your nine color samples into the nine squares in the top horizontal row you laid out with the pencil.

5. With your paints, fill the square below each color with a gray you think is its match in terms of lightness and darkness. To achieve matches that are as close as possible, try not only matching your grays to each color square, but check the intervals horizontally in the row of color squares, and try to approximate the intervals in the row of grays.

Want to see how you've done? Take your end product and reproduce it on a black-and-white photocopier. If you've nailed it, your grays should look the same as the color samples you matched them with.

Figure 1

SATURATION

CONTRAST OF PURE AND DULL

Saturation is the relative degree of purity a color exhibits. Think of contrast of saturation as the relationship between full strength and diluted, intense and dull, rich and spare (see figure 1). Think of a sponge and water as an analogy. When the sponge absorbs all the water it can, it reaches its saturation point. When it's completely dry, it's unsaturated. And there are many states in between, where the sponge is partially saturated.

A pure color consists of one hue in isolation. It's not interfered with and it's not mixed with other colors. Most colors used by designers—and virtually all our experiences of color in nature—have been somewhat neutralized or diluted. Color can be diluted in a variety of ways:

1. Mixing a color with any other color, from the purest of bright colors to the dullest of *neutral colors*, will rob the original color of some of its purity. Mixing in small amounts of the added color will result in a mildly neutral version of the original color. Mixing in larger amounts can deprive the original color of its identity altogether.

2. Adding white will bleach any color, lightening it and robbing it of intensity. Colors diluted in this way are often referred to as pastel.

Grid 1

3. Adding black will darken any color and deprive it of its purity as well.

4. Adding gray will dull any color and, depending on the value of the gray, also lighten or darken it.

5. The most direct and powerful way to rob a color of its purity is to mix it with its complement (its opposite on the color wheel). Any time the three primary colors—yellow, blue, and red—are directly or indirectly combined, a gray or "mud" is the result. In theory, mixing exact complements will produce a perfectly neutral gray. When you work with pigments used in paints, dyes, inks, ceramic glazes, and so on, complements in name are rarely exactly complementary. To produce a perfectly neutral gray, you often need to make adjustments after mixing.

Grid 1 consists of yellow, a neutral gray that's its equal in value, and a series of steps in between. Because the degree of saturation ranges from absolutely pure to absolutely dull, the arrangement is quite powerful and lively. The space is full of tension and dynamic. If this is the kind of feeling you'd like your design to evoke, consider using this kind of palette.

limited range in terms of pure and dull, the space feels naturally unified. The tension in the space is not as dramatic as in Grid 1, and its mood is relatively subdued and serene.

Compare Grid 2 to Grid 3, where the elements are all nearly pure. This design is much more dramatic. It feels very jazzy and tense. Note, too, the power of the few appearances of relatively dull color here. They stand out by virtue of their difference.

As is the case with all color contrasts, the pure-dull dynamic is a relative relationship. Compare the color in the small squares inside the large squares in figure 2. The somewhat neutralized yellow, which is exactly the same in both boxes, feels relatively pure when it's inside a field of neutral gray. On the other hand, it seems quite dull in the context of pure yellow.

Figure 2

Grid 2

Grid 3

Grid 2 shows a family of neutralized color. While most of the members are quiet (greatly neutralized), several make more noise and stand out from the rest. That's because they're relatively "colorful," or more highly saturated. Because of its

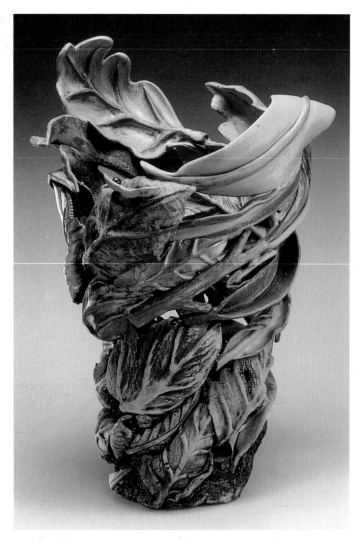

LINDA HUEY, *Wind,* 1998.
28 x 18 x 18 inches
(71.1 x 45.7 x 45.7 cm).
Handbuilt low-fire clay
with low-fire glazes.
Photo by Brian Oglesbee.

ANA LISA HEDSTROM,
Untitled, 1998.
Shibori resist dyed
and pieced silk.
Photo by Kevin Meynal.

Examples

In Linda Huey's handbuilt ceramic *Wind,* above left, a series of leaf forms move in circular fashion to create a vessel. The movement up, around, and in some cases out of the form is greatly enhanced by the play of pure against dull. At the bottom, the leaves are entirely dull gray. There's no contrast of saturation at all. As the leaves move up, they begin to exhibit bits of color—yellows and oranges—and pure notes begin to vibrate quite nicely against the gray. By the time they reach the top, the leaves are almost all yellow and orange, and quite highly saturated.

Art-to-wear composer Ana Lisa Hedstrom skillfully plays pure color against dull to achieve the very bold and graphic arrangement in her *Untitled,* above right. She starts with a completely passive and absolutely neutral ground color, midtone gray. In the context of this gray, any other color, even a fairly neutralized one, would feel relatively pure. When highly saturated colors come into play, as they do here, they really dance.

Sol LeWitt takes advantage of pure-dull contrast in his dynamic *Barolo Chapel,* facing page, top. He uses the exterior of this old chapel, set in the rural Italian landscape, as a surface for a series of wall paintings that stand in dramatic contrast to their surroundings. The chapel's pure colors are unlike their counterparts in nature, which are somewhat

SOL LEWITT,
Barolo Chapel, 1998-99.
Photo by Carlo Valsecchi.
Courtesy of Bruno and
Marcello Ceretto.

neutralized in the foreground, and appear more and more neutral as they move into the distance. The result is a mood that's lively and joyous.

Finally, notice the same principle at work in the outdoor patio environment in Martina Meyer's *Garden Seating*, right. Highly saturated color makes the pair of chaise lounges the centerpiece around which the remaining elements revolve.

MARTINA MEYER,
Garden Seating, 2000.
Landscape architecture.
Photo by artist.

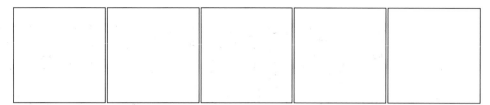

Figure 3

Exercise

FIVE-STEP SATURATION SCALE

This challenge repeats the scale format used in the Value section, this time placing pure and dull at the ends of the scale. It familiarizes you with the tools you'll use when you organize a design according to saturation contrast. The saturation scale will show a series of equal steps as a color moves from pure to dull. Again, the scale should be similar to a staircase in a house, with the intervals between steps being identical. You'll also want the surface of each square to be nice and smooth, without contrasting marks and variations. If you like, refer to the pure-dull scales on page 76 as a basic model.

What You Need

Ruler

Pencil

Flat rectangular surface (white or off white), such as a piece
    of heavyweight paper, cardboard, or mat board, at least
    12 x 6 inches (30.5 x 15.2 cm)

White paint
    (anything from acrylic craft paint to house paint to oil)

Black paint (same type you selected for the white paint)

One pure color of paint that's mid-tone in value (same type
    you selected for the white paint)

Small brush

Mixing tool

Cleaning materials (mineral spirits or turpentine for oil, water
    for other paints, and a rag)

Palette to mix paint on, such as a plastic lid

What You Do

1. To make things a bit simpler this time, we'll shorten the scale to five steps rather than nine. With the ruler and pencil,
lightly mark off a horizontal row of five adjoining squares, each 1 x 1 inch (2.5 x 2.5 cm) (see figure 3). Above each square, number 1 through 5 from left to right.

2. Fill in square number 1 with an absolutely solid coating of the pure, middle-value color you selected.

3. With the white and black paint, mix a gray that's equal in value to the pure color you're using. Refer back to the color-to-value translation challenge in the last chapter, page 74, if you need to.

4. Fill in square number 5 with a smooth, solid coating of the gray you mixed.

5. Using your pure color and the gray you mixed as its value equal, mix a dulled version of your color that you judge to be halfway between your pure color and your gray.

6. Fill in square number 3 with the dulled version you just mixed.

7. Using the pure color in square 1 and the dulled color in square 3, mix an even duller version of your color, one that you judge to be halfway between the pure in square 1 and the mid-dull in square 3. Fill in square 2 with this fairly pure color.

8. Using the gray in square 5 and the mid-dull in square 3, mix a very dull version of the color, one that you judge to be halfway between the dull in square 5 and the mid-dull color in square 3. Fill in square 4 with this very neutralized color.

9. Moving one step at a time across the scale, isolate groupings of three in a row (you might cover the rest of the squares with pieces of paper), and check to see if some of the pure-dull intervals seem to be bigger or smaller than the rest, and make adjustments. Your goal: five even steps, like a stairway in a house.

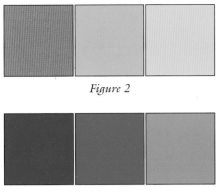

Figure 2

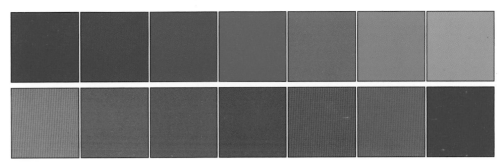

Figure 1

Figure 3

TEMPERATURE

CONTRAST OF WARM AND COOL

A color's *temperature* has to do with how warm or cold it makes you feel. The relationships between relative warmth and coolness in an arrangement create contrast of temperature (see figure 1).

Warm colors are generally agreed to be those in the red-orange-yellow family (see figure 2). They're the colors associated with things like fire, heat, and sun. Cool colors are the opposites of the warm ones on the wheel, the green-blue-purple family (see figure 3). They might be associated with iciness, cold water, or a crystalline blue sky. Everything else being equal, warm colors generally have a "coming forward" feeling. We view them as asserting themselves. Cool colors, on the other hand, recede in our vision. Designers often take advantage of this advancing-receding aspect of the warm-cool relationship to create the illusion of depth on a two-dimensional surface or to create a feeling of vibration.

When you contrast complementary (opposite) colors, which we'll discuss more in the next section, you can send a variety of warm-cool messages. The orange-blue complementary contrast is always one of warm (orange) contrasted with cool (blue). The yellow-purple complementary contrast is always one of warm (yellow) contrasted with cool (purple). The red-green complementary contrast is almost always warm (red) contrasted with cool (green), though at times it may be too close to call. A hot green, for example, that leans very much toward yellow may appear equal in temperature or even warmer when placed next to a very cool red that leans toward purple.

Contrast of temperature can also be used to create mood. Though reactions to colors are somewhat subjective and

different from culture to culture, general tendencies apply. Arrangements dominated by cool colors typically evoke feelings of peace, quiet, serenity, and tranquility. Warm color arrangements often bring about feelings that are relatively active and dynamic, from vivacity and joy to anger.

Finally, when looking at contrast of temperature, it's important to remember that other visual forces can make elements advance or recede, too, and they can overrule the warm-cool dynamic. In addition, the qualities of warm and cool with respect to color are relative. Just as we need dark to experience light and dullness to experience intensity, we experience warmth in relation to coolness, and vice versa. Therefore, keep in mind that a color that seems warm when surrounded by cooler colors can seem cool if it's surrounded by warmer ones (see figure 4).

Figure 4

Grid 1

Grid 2

Grid 1 shows what occurs in a design when its character is predominately cold, and a few relatively warm notes pull our eye in and around the space. Because the temperature range here is quite narrow, the design seems to hold together naturally. The limited range in temperature also means there's a minimum of color tension in the space. The resulting mood is orderly, tranquil, and serene.

Grid 2, on the other hand, is also a predominately cold space, but it uses the full range of temperature in the palette. Here, the stark cold blue is played against green, which, in this context, feels quite warm. This design is much more dramatic. Its tensions are much more lively, and the mood more exciting and dynamic.

Examples

Coral Waves, by Annette W. Bower, facing page, top left, is a textbook illustration of how warm-cold contrast works. Bower plays warm red against cold blue, with virtually no other contrast in the design.

Cool colors dominate *Blue Ode to Judy O*, by Jackie Abrams, facing page, top right. A variety of blues, greens, and purples cover the vast majority of the woven basket's surface. Little flickers of heat—oranges, yellows, and reds—are interspersed throughout, creating a pattern of surface vibration. They push forward, while the cool passages recede.

Marilyn McKenzie Chaffee's quilted *Crystal Medallion*, facing page, bottom left, is a good example of contrast of temperature in a design with more neutralized color. Warm browns that vary in purity and value play against a series of neutral grays that feel quite cool in relation to the browns.

Landscape architect Signe Nielsen uses a similar palette, though with slightly more purity in color, in a garden floor arrangement, facing page, bottom right. She plays the cool blue notes of the Mexican beach pebbles against the warm accents of the soil. To create a dialogue between the two, she introduces brownstone pavers inside the cool pebble bed.

ANNETTE W. BOWER, *Coral Waves,* 2000. 24 inches (61 cm). Beaded spiral rope and branch fringe. *Photo by Jerry Anthony. Collection of Barbara Chadwick.*

JACKIE ABRAMS, *Blue Ode to Judy O,* 1993. 5 x 13 x 13 inches (12.7 x 33 x 33 cm). Basket woven of painted cotton paper. *Photo by Charley Freiberg.*

MARILYN MCKENZIE CHAFFEE, *Crystal Medallion,* 1984. 55 x 55 inches (139.7 x 139.7 cm). Cotton fabrics, polyester batting; machine pieced, hand quilted. *Photo by artist.*

SIGNE NIELSEN, 1990. 35 x 75 feet (10.5 x 22.5 m). Courtyard; cut square bluestone 2 inches (5 cm) thick, Mexican beach pebbles. *Photo by James R. Morse.*

MARY MAXTION, *Log Cabin,* 1994. 88 x 73 inches (223.5 x 185.4 cm). Quilt.
Collection of the International Quilt Study Center, University of Nebraska-Lincoln
(accession number 2000.04.0080).

"Sky Chicken Sprouts Power Wings"   Renie

RENIE BRESKIN ADAMS, *Sky Chicken Sprouts Power Wings,* 2001.
6⅝ x 6⅛ inches (16.8 x 15.5 cm). Hand embroidered cotton. *Photo by artist. Collection of artist.*

At first, you might not even recognize the warm-cold contrast in Mary Maxtion's *Log Cabin*, above left. Her design is composed of a grid-like crisscrossing of horizontal and vertical linear movements in red. Small green squares mark their points of intersection. Underneath this red-green grid is a series of partial squares in various colors and orientations. They push forward and pull back against the grid, creating a dynamic feeling. So where is the contrast of warm and cold, and how is it crucial to the organization of the design? It's in the contrast in temperature among the little green squares at the surface grid's intersections. Notice how the very warm

yellowish green squares pop out and establish the surface grid as dominant. At the same time, the deep, cool, bluish green squares want to recede into the space. The push-and-pull, front-and-back, warm-cool dialogue among the greens creates the spatial vibration that makes Maxtion's arrangement so compelling.

Renie Breskin Adams uses contrast of temperature to establish degrees of emphasis and rhythmic movement in *Sky Chicken Sprouts Power Wings*, above right. The design's forms float on top of a ground that's rich in cool purples, blues, and blue greens. Each of the forms offers some heat to contrast with the ground. The hottest element—and therefore the primary point of emphasis—is the pure yellow chicken, who also has a warm red headdress and "sprouted" wings, which are predominately warm—and mighty big. The remaining four figures and the warm notes they contain play supporting roles. Together, they create a rhythmic movement that frames the chicken.

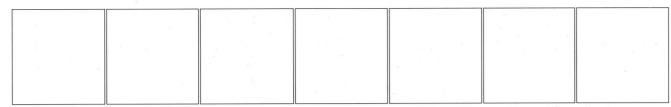

Figure 5

Exercise

SEVEN-STEP WARM-COOL SCALE

We'll continue working in the scale format, this time to practice plotting out contrast of temperature. The warm-cool scale will have a relative cool on one end and a relative warm on the other, and show a movement of equal steps as the color changes temperature. To best illustrate contrast of temperature, work with three colors that are each a step apart on the color wheel.

What You Need

Ruler

Pencil

Surface to paint on, such as heavyweight paper, cardboard, or mat board, at least 12 x 6 inches (30.5 x 15.2 cm)

White paint
(anything from acrylic craft paint to house paint to oil)

Blue paint (same type as you selected for the white paint)

Green paint (same type) that is midtone in value

Yellow paint (same type)

Small brush

Mixing tool

Cleaning materials (mineral spirits or turpentine for oil, water for other paints, and a rag)

Palette to mix paint on, such as a plastic lid

What You Do

1. With the ruler and pencil, lightly mark off a horizontal row of seven adjoining squares, each 1 x 1 inch (2.5 x 2.5 cm) (see figure 5). Above each square, number 1 through 7 from left to right.

2. Put some blue, green, and yellow paint on your palette.

3. Mix green with yellow to get a yellow green that you judge to be halfway between the pure yellow and pure green.

4. To eliminate any value contrast from the colors in this scale, mix some white with both the pure green and the pure blue, so they're both equal in value to the yellow green.

5. Fill in square number 1 with a smooth and even coating of the yellow green.

6. Fill in square number 7 with a smooth and even coating of the lightened blue.

7. From the yellow green and the lightened blue, mix a color that you judge to be halfway between the two, and fill in square number 4.

8. From the yellow green and the color in square 4, mix two variations that will be equal steps in a three-step movement from number 1 to number 4. Fill in squares 2 and 3 with the two colors.

9. From the lightened blue and the color in square 4, mix two variations that will represent equal steps in a three-step movement from number 4 to number 7. Fill in squares 5 and 6 with the two colors.

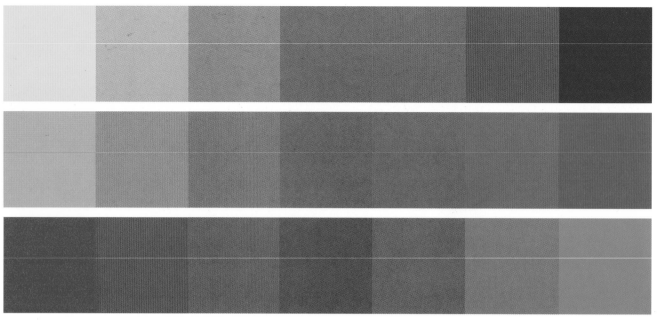

Figure 1

COMPLEMENTS

CONTRAST OF OPPOSITE COLORS

Complementary colors are those situated opposite each other on the color wheel. They create powerful and complex relationships in a design. Figure 1 shows the range of color you might use. When one is placed next to or near the other, complementary colors enhance one another. Each encourages its opposite toward maximum vividness.

Complements relate in a way that calls on all three primary colors to work together. Complementary pairs are made up of one primary color and one secondary color. The secondary color is a mix of the other two primary colors. So, the whole color wheel is engaged in a complementary pair, lending a feeling of unity and completeness to the color arrangement.

Ironically, complements also stand in opposition to each other. When they're mixed together or transparently layered over one another, they dull each other, each diminishing the power and identity of the other. Taken to the extreme, a perfectly proportioned mixture of absolute complements brings about a total obliteration of color, resulting in a perfectly neutral gray.

Want another indicator of how powerful the complementary relationship is? When you look at a color, any color, in a color-neutral context (such as white, gray, or black), your eye reflexively wants to see that color's complement. In fact, it will generate an experience of its complement. Look at figures 2 and 3 to see this for yourself. You see small squares of a perfectly neutral gray (each gray is the same), presented

Figure 2

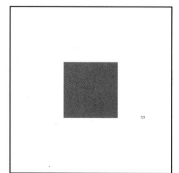

Figure 3

inside larger squares of white and of pure color. Look at each of these squares-inside-squares one at a time; you might want to cover the others with your hands or a piece of paper. Compare the gray inside a pure color with the adjacent gray surrounded by white. You'll begin to read the gray square inside pure color as having a tinge of the complement of the pure color. The gray inside the yellow, for example, gives the faint impression of purple; the gray inside the blue takes on a hint of orange. Color theorists refer to this phenomenon as *simultaneous contrast*.

Finally, note that each complementary pairing inherently involves other color contrasts as well:

• The orange-blue pairing, for example, always involves extreme warm-cold contrast (pure blue, after all, always plays as cool, regardless of context).

• The yellow-purple contrast always includes extreme light-dark contrast as part of the relationship.

• The red-green relationship is most often a warm-cold one, though green leaning strongly toward yellow may be as warm as red leaning strongly toward purple.

Grid 1 features the full range of colors present in a scale of complements. It uses colors from both ends of the scale and shows how complementary contrast functions in its most lively and dynamic state.

Grid 2, on the other hand, shows a design that's unified by a lot of one color and a small amount of its complement.

Grid 1

Grid 2

BONNIE SEEMAN, *Hojala,* 2000. 8 x 8 x 7 inches
(20.3 x 20.3 x 17.8 cm). Porcelain. *Photo by artist.*

ROBIN CAMPO, *Chop Pot,* 1999. 16 x 7 x 15 inches
(40.6 x 17.8 x 38.1 cm). Earthenware. *Photo by artist.*

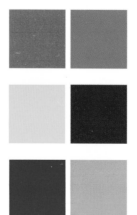

The three pairs of
complementary colors

Examples

Bonnie Seeman's contemporary ceramic teapot *Hojala,* above
left, is a clear example of red-green complementary contrast
at work. Light and dark greens activate the lower passages
and act in supportive contrast to the complementary red in
the larger forms above.

The delightfully unorthodox *Chop Pot,* by Robin Campo,
above right, provides a fine example of a design organized
around the yellow-purple complementary contrast. The yellow
enlivens and completes the purple, the purple does the same
for the yellow, and both colors are enlivened by their pureness
in relation to the dull grays.

Three photographic designs that combine architectural details
and elements of sky show how exciting and dynamic complementary contrast can be. In Dana Irwin's *Oaxaca
Rooftops,* facing page, top left, the blue-orange complementary relationship rules. These colors—in highly saturated

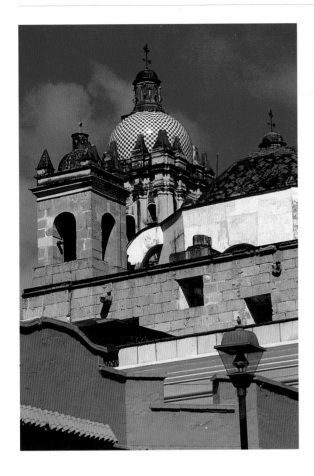

DANA IRWIN, *Oaxaca Rooftops,* 2002.

DANA IRWIN, *Oaxaca Color,* 2002.

SKIP WADE, *Untitled,* 2003. Color photograph of a temple in the Old Town Section of Hoi An, Vietnam.

form—play off one another clearly and beautifully in the geometric architectural passages at the bottom of the arrangement. What makes the composition rich and intriguing is the way that relatively dull, orange-like notes in the bronze and tile elements above play against the deep, rich blues in the sky. These contrasting versions of the complementary pairing make for a rich and compelling color experience. Irwin's *Oaxaca Color,* above center, also explores the blue-orange dynamic. This time, blue is dominant, enabling the one prominent orange element, the door, to function as the focal point of the design. Relatively minor appearances of orange in the space—in the metal window cover grate and in the line of the roofing tiles above—encourage the eye to journey around the design in a satisfying way. Finally, Skip Wade's photograph, above right, embraces the red-green complementary contrast to unify the arrangement. At the same time, reds vary in value and saturation while greens vary in temperature, resulting in wonderful chromatic variety and tension.

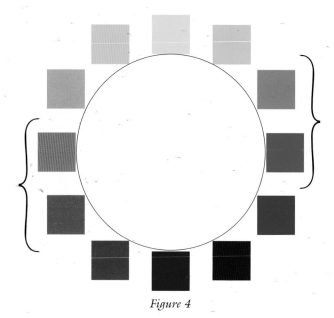

Figure 4

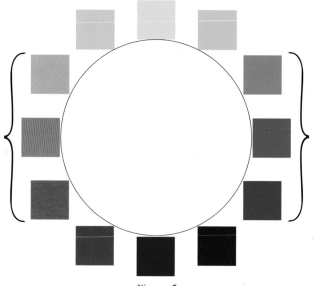

Figure 5

Designs can be organized strictly around one complementary pair, as we have just seen. Very often, however, designers use an expanded version of this idea, extending the complementary colors to include adjacent colors on the wheel. For example, the red-green complementary pair can be expanded to include colors one-half step either way. Go to one side, and your palette consists of reds that vary from pure red to red orange, and greens that vary from pure green to green blue (see figure 4). Technically, you're now working with two sets of complements: red/green and red orange/green blue. Go in the opposite direction on the wheel, and you'll be working with reds that range from pure red to red purple and greens that range from pure green to green yellow. Your two sets of complements are now red/green and red purple/green yellow. You can even work with all of these variations simultaneously, or with adjacents that are two steps apart (see figure 5). Whichever possibility you choose, you're designing using extensions of the red-green theme. These extensions open possibilities for richer, broader arrangements that still create a strong feeling of unity.

Richard Box extends red-green complementary contrast to include a full range of adjacents in his fiber composition *Poppies and Daisies*, left.

In *Koi Kimono*, facing page, right, art-to-wear designer Tim Harding arranges very intense blues and oranges, so they excite one another and produce great tension and, at the same time, complete one another and evoke a feeling of resolution. The warm orange elements—ranging from nearly yellow to nearly red—dance and dart across the space, while vibrating in and out of the vast cool, complementary blue ground. The blues exhibit a rich range as well. Some are dark, some midtone, others light. Some are very cool, leaning almost to purple; others are nearly green.

RICHARD BOX, *Poppies and Daisies,* 1986. 10 x 6 inches (25.4 x 15.2 cm). Fabric collage with machine and hand embroidery. *Photo by artist.*

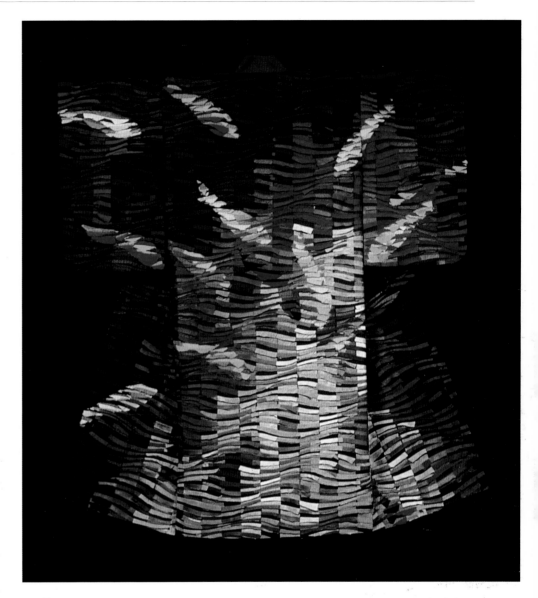

Finally, for a look at a design organized around two complementary pairs, consider Kathran Siegel's chair composition *Yellow Swirl*, above left. At first glance, this arrangement might seem to be based on a simple yellow-purple complementary contrast. The pair does dominate, but a closer look reveals a secondary blue-orange complementary contrast in the design. Siegel uses blues on the narrow zigzag forms on the right side of the seat and on the narrow front faces of the legs. She contrasts this with the dull orange brown of the large, unpainted wood areas throughout. These delightfully unexpected color relationships establish a playfully quirky mood.

KATHRAN SIEGEL,
Yellow Swirl, 1986.
48 x 22 x 22 inches
(121.9 x 55.9 x 55.9 cm).
Laminated, carved, painted
maple. *Photo by artist.*

TIM HARDING, *Koi Kimono,*
1996. 68 x 64 x 3 inches
(172.7 x 162.6 x 7.6 cm).
Collaged, layered, stitched,
cut, pressed silks.
Photo by Petronella Ytsma.

■ EXERCISE 1

COMPLEMENTARY SCALE IN PAINT

This scale gives you practice with the tools you'll use when complementary contrast is your organizing principle. It includes not only a pairing of pure complements, but a pairing of partially neutralized counterparts as well, since complementary contrast can be active in cases of both pure and dull color. Again, in keeping with the scales in previous sections, this one should be like a staircase, with the intervals being equal and the surfaces smooth and consistent.

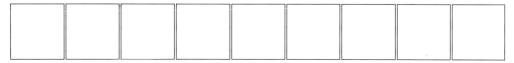

Figure 6

What You Need

Surface to paint on, such as heavyweight paper, cardboard, or mat board, at least a 12 x 6 inches (30.5 x 15.2 cm)

White paint
   (anything from acrylic craft paint to house paint to oil)

Black paint (same type as you selected for the white paint)

Red paint (same type)

Green paint (same type)

Small brush

Mixing tool

Cleaning materials (mineral spirits or turpentine for oil, water for other paints, and a rag)

Palette to mix paint on, such as a plastic lid

Ruler

Pencil

What You Do

1. With the ruler and pencil, lightly mark off a horizontal row of nine adjoining squares, each 1 x1 inch (2.5 x 2.5 cm) (see figure 6). Above each square, number 1 through 9 from left to right.

2. Put some red, green, white, and black paint on the palette.

3. Determine whether the red or the green is lighter in value (if necessary, refer back to the color-to-value translation exercises, page 74). With the white and black paint, mix a gray that is its equal in value.

4. Mix a little white with the red or the green, so its value is equal to the gray and its lighter complement.

5. Fill in square number 1 with the red.

6. Fill in square number 9 with the green.

7. Fill in square number 5 with the gray.

8. Mix the red with the gray to get a dulled red, halfway between the pure red and the gray, and use it to fill in square 3.

9. Mix the green with the gray to get a dulled green, halfway between the pure green and the gray, and use it to fill in square 7.

10. Mix the paints used in squares 1 and 3 to get a color halfway between for square 2. Mix the paints used in squares 3 and 5 to get a color halfway between for square 4. Mix the paints used in squares 5 and 7 to get a color halfway between for square 6. And mix the paints used in squares 7 and 9 to get a color halfway between for square 8.

■ EXERCISE 2

COMPLEMENTARY PAIR SCALES

This exercise creates two parallel scales that illustrate the palette you'll use when designing with complementary pairs.

What You Need

Ruler

Pencil

Surface to paint on, such as heavyweight paper, cardboard, or mat board, at least 12 x 6 inches (30.5 x 15.2 cm)

White paint
   (anything from acrylic craft paint to house paint to oil)

Black paint (same type you selected for the white paint)

Red paint (same type)

Orange paint (same type)

Green paint (same type)

Blue Paint (same type)

Small brush

Mixing tool

Cleaning materials (mineral spirits or turpentine for oil, water for other paints, and a rag)

Palette to mix paint on, such as a plastic lid

What You Do

1. With the ruler and pencil, lightly mark off two horizontal rows, one on top of the other, of five adjoining squares, each 1 x 1 inch (2.5 x 2.5 cm) (see figure 7). Above each square, number 1 through 5 from left to right.

2. Put some red, orange, green, blue, white, and black paint on the palette.

3. Determine which one of the four colors is the lightest in value and, with the white and black paint, mix a gray that is its equal in value.

4. Mix a little white with the remaining colors to lighten them, so the value of each is equal to the gray.

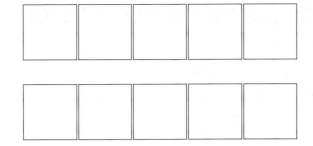

Figure 7

ON THE TOP ROW OF SQUARES:

1. Fill in square number 1 with the pure red.

2. Fill in square number 5 with the pure green.

3. Fill in square number 3 with the gray.

4. Mix the pure red with the gray to get a dulled red, halfway between the pure red and the gray, and use it to fill in square 2.

5. Mix the pure green with the gray to get a dulled green, halfway between the pure green and the gray, and use it to fill in square 4.

ON THE BOTTOM ROW OF SQUARES:

1. Mix the red and the orange to get a red orange halfway between the two, and use it to fill in square 1.

2. Mix the green and the blue to get a blue green halfway between the two, and use it to fill in square 5.

3. Fill in square number 3 with the gray.

4. Mix the red orange with the gray to get a dulled red orange, halfway between the pure red orange and the gray, and use it to fill in square 2.

5. Mix the pure blue green with the gray to get a dulled blue green, halfway between the pure blue green and the gray, and use it to fill in square 4.

CHAPTER 4

THE DESIGN SPACE

We've covered the purposes and processes of design and the visual elements you'll use as raw materials in creating your design. What you need to consider next is the nature of the space you'll arrange those elements in.

Essentially, design spaces come in two forms: flat, two-dimensional spaces that can be anything from canvases and billboards to swatches of fabric, and three-dimensional spaces, such as blocks of wood, pieces of stone, or environments, from room interiors to areas in a landscape. Of course, there are hybrids of the two, and sometimes it can be difficult to neatly label the finished design—if it's a thick, multilayered collage on a flat piece of paper, is it two dimensional or three dimensional? The following works as a general rule. Designs meant to be viewed from one direction are primarily two dimensional. If you need to view a design from more than one direction to fully take it in, it's three dimensional.

There are important differences between working in two and three dimensions. In two dimensions you arrange shapes, while in three dimensions you work with forms. In three dimensions you have to think "in the round," always considering how your design works when viewed from many directions at once. You need to treat depth and gravity in different ways as well. In three dimensions, there's actual depth of space (forms are actually in front of and behind one another) and actual gravity (forms will fall when insufficiently supported). In two-dimensional design, you don't have these dynamics to contend with, though you can create the illusion of depth or the feeling of gravity on your flat surface.

These differences aside, two- and three-dimensional design spaces have much in common. The visual elements you use in them are the same, as are the ways you can arrange them. And both kinds of design spaces feature the same internal dynamics that affect how your design works. Once you're aware of those dynamics, you can consider their impact and work with them to create the design you want. The rest of this chapter provides an overview of them.

TOP VS. BOTTOM

Visual elements feel very different when they're placed near the top of a design space as opposed to near the bottom. Everything else being equal, the eye notices elements placed high in a space first. Consider a shape of color, for example. Placed near the top of a design space, the shape feels prominent, elevated, and active. It feels as if it's about to move or fall. Since we tend to read two-dimensional design spaces as landscapes or room interiors, a shape near the top seems to be defying gravity by staying up high without any visible means of support or propulsion (see figure 1). On the other hand, placed near the bottom, the same shape of color feels less prominent; the eye is less likely to go to it first. But it also feels relatively stable, still, and supported. It's as if the shape is sitting on the floor or a tabletop (see figure 2).

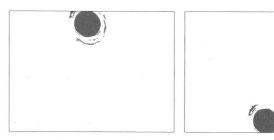

Figure 1   *Figure 2*

A design with most of its major forces at the top feels active and dynamic, while a design with activity clustered near the bottom feels relatively stable and grounded. Fran Skiles's *Red Landscape* quilt is shown at the top of the facing page right side up (left) and upside down (right). In both orientations there's an elongated, vertical shape containing light elements that stands out from the rest of the design, which is dark and relatively passive. In the right-side-up orientation, the cluster of light elements rests comfortably and solidly on the bottom. It feels grounded, stable, and in place. Individual elements near the top of this shape tend to stand out. Look at the design turned upside down, and the effect is quite different. The shape of light elements moves mainly to the upper half of the space, and the eye goes right to it. It's highly energized, resulting in a design that's much more dynamic.

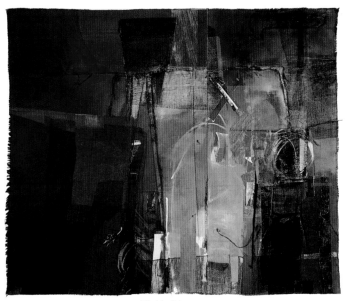

FRAN SKILES,
Red Landscape, 1996.
52 x 63 inches
(132.1 x 160 cm).
Cotton duck fabric, woven
printed hemp, treated with oil
stick, acrylic, and fabric paint;
machine stitched.
Photo by Gerhard Heidersberger.

Right side up.

Upside down.

LEFT VS. RIGHT

We have a tendency to look at the left of a design space before the right (see figures 3 and 4). The reflex is likely cultural—in western culture, we begin reading at the left of a page.

Look at Nöel Ruessmann's fiber composition *Autumn Leaves Triptych* in its right-side-up orientation, below left. Look away, and then back at it, and notice that your eye goes to the leaf in the upper left, to the purple fragment in the middle next, and finally to the circular elements on the right. In the upside-down version, below right, the eye is drawn to the large leaf in the upper left before the smaller leaf on the right. As a result of this left-then-right reflex, the overall feeling of Ruessmann's design space is very different in the two orientations. In the original, the experience begins with two panels that are light, open, and airy before settling in the third panel, which is much darker and more dense. The overall feeling is airy and fluid. In the flipped orientation, the experience begins with a dark, dense bar we have to fight through before reaching the open and airy passages. The overall design feels heavier and more static.

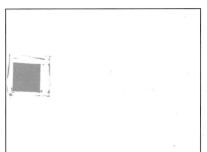

Figure 3

Figure 4

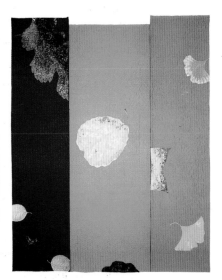

NOËL M. RUESSMANN, *Autumn Leaves Triptych,* 2000.
76 x 61 x ¼ inches (193 x 154.9 x .6 cm). Appliqué leaves embellished with acrylic paint; hand quilted. *Photo by Joe Mikuliak.*

Right side up.

Upside down.

UPPER LEFT VS. BOTTOM RIGHT

If we tend to experience the top before the bottom and the left before the right, then all else being equal, we'll begin our experience of a design space in the upper left. Elements placed in the upper left become more powerful and prominent there than they would be in any other placement. Conversely, the lower right placement is, on first glance, the least powerful and prominent location in a design space (see figures 5 and 6).

Figure 5

Figure 6

Rembrandt's *Susanna Surprised by the Elders*, below left, illustrates this principle nicely as well. Notice how a little wedge of light placed on the edge in the upper left corner and pointed to by the diagonal thrust of the woman's torso is enough of a weight to offset a seemingly much more powerful cluster of elements at the bottom right.

Ironically, placing elements in the lower right also has design advantages. It's the location where viewers tend to pause, consider, and conclude their experiences. To see this principle at work, look through any magazine and notice just how many print advertisements have logos or summary slogans in the bottom right corner. Consider the movie poster, below right, in which the name of its superstar appears in the lower right corner.

CENTER

The exact center of a design space is both a very powerful and absolutely static placement (see figure 7). A design element here is equidistant from top and bottom, left and right.

Figure 7

CONTINENTAL LITHO CORP., *Bordertown,* 1934. Movie poster. Copyright by Vitagraph, Inc. Used with permission of Warner Bros. Productions Corp. Picture. Image courtesy of the Library of Congress.

REMBRANDT VAN RIJN, *Susanna Surprised by the Elders,* 1647. 30 1/8 x 36 1/2 inches (76.5 x 92.8 cm). Oil on panel. Photo Joerg P. Anders. Gemäldegalerie, Berlin, Germany.

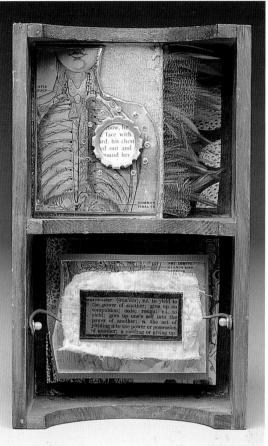

Center is the only placement that creates no contrasting spatial tensions for the eye to distinguish. Because of this, the exact center placement can create a somewhat awkward and disorienting feeling, and designers often avoid it.

On the other hand, exact center placement is absolutely essential in designs arranged according to radial symmetry. Linda Arndt's ceramic form *Kaleidoscope for David*, above left, is an excellent example. Notice how all of Arndt's shapes, colors, and textures are mirrored from side to side, top to bottom, and on diagonals. Most importantly, these mirrored elements radiate around and from the circular shapes in the exact center of the form. The result is a very comfortable, resolved, absolutely balanced arrangement.

NEAR CENTER

Near center is typically the most comfortable placement in a design space (see figure 8). The element you put there is close enough to center to garner attention and to enjoy comfortable relationships with other elements anywhere in the space. It's also far enough away from the middle to create a variety of tensions. Designers who want to highlight a particular element often put that element in near-center placement. In traditional portraits, for example, the head of the subject is often placed there. In many narrative designs, you'll find the primary subject just off center, as well. Nicole Tuggle places a round element containing narrative text near center in *Surrender*, above right.

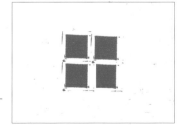

Figure 8

OUTSIDE EDGES

ERIK A. WOLKEN,
All Mixed Up, 2001.
18 x 28 x 12 inches
(46 x 71 x 30 cm).
Baltic birch plywood,
mahogany, maple, milk paint.
Photo by Seth Tice-Lewis.

Probably the most powerful placement for a visual element is on the outside edge. Anytime an element engages an edge, it challenges or embraces the space it's in. Figure 9 shows an arrangement of five simple shapes in a space. Figure 10 shows the same shapes in the same space with one very small change. One of the shapes has moved ever so slightly so it engages an edge. Notice how much more prominent and powerful it becomes?

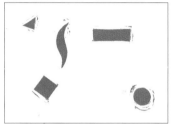

Figure 9

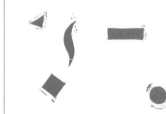

Figure 10

Lynn Whipple's *Climb*, below, shows this principle at work. Among a wide array of elements, one is crucial to the success of the design: the little square sitting on a diagonal at the right edge, near the middle. While several elements flirt with engaging the edge, only a few actually do. The square grabs at the edge much more assertively than the others; it

LYNN WHIPPLE, *Climb,*
2000. 32 x 32 x 2 inches
(81.3 x 81.3 x 5.1 cm).
Acrylic and pencil on wood,
with collage underneath.
Photo by Randall Smith.

KATHARINA KEOGHAN,
Street Dance, 1999.
11 x 16 inches
(27.9 x 40.6 cm).
Acrylic on paper.
Photo by artist.

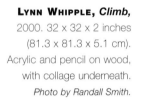

clearly goes off the edge, rather than just nicking it. As a result, it's unexpectedly powerful, pulling strongly to the right side to counter the large shape on the left.

In Katharina Keoughan's floral composition *Street Dance*, above, all of the edges of the design space are engaged by strong value contrasts, encouraging you to move from one point of engagement to the next. The movement frames the elements in the interior. Keoughan's design illustrates another principle, too. When two or more elements grab onto the same edge, they not only share the edge, they split the dividends. Neither is as powerful as it would be if it had the edge all to itself. She takes advantage of this phenomenon and uses it to balance her design. The upper areas are more highly active, with diagonals leaning to the upper right. In response, she allows only one strong element to engage the bottom, slightly to the left of center.

Virtually all the most powerful notes on the front face of Erik A. Wolken's *All Mixed Up*, facing page, top, are on the outside edge. Five dark partial circles run off the edge, pulling our attention to the outside parameters of the space and giving the box a sense of monumental significance.

CREATING DEPTH IN TWO-DIMENSIONAL SPACES

In two-dimensional design, there's no actual depth, but you can arrange visual elements in a variety of ways so that they appear to move from front to back, creating the illusion of depth.

CONVERGENCE

Arrange elements so their common directional energies meet in one area. Figure 11 shows how straight and curved lines can be used this way. Figure 12 shows how shapes can accomplish the same thing.

Suzanne J.E. Tourtillott uses convergence in *Dystopia*, above. She crops her view of this rooftop landscape so a number of architectural lines meet at a small, dark doorway in the distance. As a result, we're drawn deep into the space. Convergence creates the same kind of illusion in Herbert Matter's *All Roads Lead to Switzerland*, right.

SUZANNE J.E. TOURTILLOTT, *Dystopia,* 1982. Approx. 1 x 1⅜ inches (28 x 36 mm). Black and white direct positive film.

HERBERT MATTER, *All Roads Lead to Switzerland,* 1935. Color poster. *Courtesy of the Library of Congress.*

Figure 11   *Figure 12*

OVERLAP

When one shape overlaps another, it creates the feeling that it occupies space in front of the shape it overlaps (see figure 13).

Figure 13

TRANSPARENCY

Veiled elements, created by placing a transparent element in front or on top of another, also give the illusion of depth.

Wearable art designers Robin McKay and Ellen Marsh use *transparency* repeatedly in *Magic Geometry in Natural*, below. Transparent fabrics are layered, veiling one another and portions of the dress form underneath, causing the series of repeated geometrical shapes to vibrate forward and back.

CONTRASTS

As a general rule, when you look at a landscape or atmosphere, you see more pronounced contrasts in objects closer to you—houses or trees, for example. In the art world, this is called *atmospheric perspective*. Elements that are farther away—perhaps distant hills or sky—present contrasts that are relatively weak and less dramatic. You can use this idea of combining strong contrasts that come forward with weak contrasts that recede to create the illusion of depth in a design.

ELLEN MARSH AND ROBIN McKAY,
Magic Geometry in Natural (Transparencies Collection),
1998. Discharge paste printed, clamped, and resist dyed silk organza; black silk georgette tank dress.
Photo by Wit McKay.

• Contrast of scale. Larger shapes generally read as closer, while smaller ones seem farther away (see figure 14). Large and small marks or thick and thin lines provide the same sort of contrast.

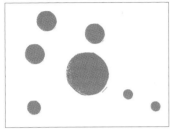

Figure 14

Figure 15

• Contrast of active and passive. Generally, passages that are more highly active come forward in our vision, while relatively quiet passages recede (see figure 15).

Figure 16

• Contrast of edge. If all else is equal, shapes defined by hard, crisp, definite edges seem nearer than shapes with relatively soft and indefinite edges (see figure 16).

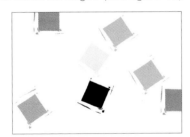

Figure 17

• Contrast of value. Relationships between strong lights and darks will bring elements forward, while relationships of midtone grays will make elements recede in comparison (see figure 17).

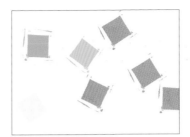

Figure 18

• Contrast of warm and cool. Contrasting color temperatures can push elements front and back. Warm colors (yellow, orange, red) feel closer; cool colors (purple, blue, green) seem to recede into space (see figure 18).

Figure 19

• Contrast of pure and dull. Pure colors come forward, while dull ones recede (see figure 19).

Gary Bolding's *Loaves and Fishes*, below, is a textbook example of using heightened contrast to create the illusion of depth. White bread and fishing lures alternate in a horizontal row, floating across the surface. They hover over land and in front of the sky. Notice how the lightest lights in the arrangement are in the rolls and lures, while the distant clouds are completely middle value. Notice how the purest of colors are in the floating objects, and so are the sharpest edges. Bolding ever so slightly softened the edge between sky and earth, so the floating objects stand out more still.

GARY BOLDING,
Loaves and Fishes,
1993. 5½ x 31 inches (14 x 78.7 cm). Oil on wood. *Collection of Steven Smith*.

PRINCIPLES

OF

ARRANGEMENT

The six chapters that follow explore the most fundamental principle of visual arrangement: *unity and variety.* Artists from all cultures, throughout time, and regardless of media use this principle in their designs. You can carefully plan your compositions with this idea in mind. Or, as is more often the case, if your design doesn't seem to be working in a satisfying way, you can troubleshoot by checking to see how well the principle is at work—and perhaps find a solution to your problem.

Unity and variety means that the design elements in a space relate with enough coherency to hold the space together and enough diversity to make things interesting. The unifying element may be shape, color, texture, mark, rhythm, scale, or placement. Variations in those forces—or through the introduction of contrasting forces—can give a design some necessary tension. In fact, it's often the presence of forces that don't quite fit that makes a design interesting, compelling, even mysterious.

Real-world designers rarely set out to organize a composition around only one way of achieving unity and variety. Designs usually revolve around several simultaneously, and they typically involve organization according to color as well. Most often, however, one of the six principles described in the following chapters can be considered the primary organizer of a design.

CHAPTER 5

REPETITION OF MOTIF

One of the simplest and most universal ways to organize a design is to use *repetition of motif*. Once you become aware of it, you'll notice this principle at play in designs of all kinds, everywhere you look.

Repetition means the obvious: the motif recurs throughout the design. A *motif* in a visual design is a primary element, most often a shape or color. Shape motifs include ovals, rectangles, triangles, figure eights, the letter R, the numeral 7 ... the possibilities are endless. And any color can serve as a motif. Other visual elements, such as texture and mark, can, too.

Imagine a design based on the repetition of an oval. The space is *unified* because it contains members of the same shape family. To create *variety* or visual tension and make the space more active, you can introduce ovals that vary in a number of ways: scale (bigger and smaller), width (fatter and thinner), completeness (whole and fragmentary), relative position (overlapping, touching, near one another, isolated); you get the idea. You can also add non-oval shapes to the composition to contrast with the motif and add more interest and variation.

Compare this idea to music. What pops into your head when you think of Beethoven's Fifth Symphony? Probably *dadadaDUM, dadadaDUM. That's* a motif—a very fundamental and simple cluster of four notes. When taken together, they form the primary event on which the symphony is based. For the rest of the work, Beethoven goes on at length

about dadadaDUM, repeating it while introducing an extraordinary array of variations and modifications. The result is enormously satisfying. When you're working with the idea of repetition of motif, think about exploring a visual motif in the same way that Beethoven explored dadadaDUM, and you'll be on the right track.

JUDY GLASSER,
Carved Vase, 1997.
12 x 15 x 6 inches
(30.5 x 38.1 x 15.2 cm).
Stoneware. *Photo by Theresa Schwiendt.*

Examples

Carved Vase, above, a slab-built stoneware form by Judy Glasser, is an excellent example of a design based on a circle. The fact that the circles on its surface are all similar in

DON GUREWITZ, *Fulani Wedding Earrings,* 1999. Color photograph taken in Senosa, Mali. *Collection of the artist.*

size and are carved in roughly the same way adds to the feeling of unity. Variations occur when the circles appear in a fragmentary form as they trail off the base and move partially out of view, disappearing around the three-dimensional form. Partial circles appear again in the shape of the handles. To finish it off, the vessel's curved top forms another partial circle.

The Western African woman in Don Gurewitz's documentary photograph *Fulani Wedding Earrings*, above, is adorned in fabric and jewelry that repeat a dynamic circular motif as well. Dramatically oversized, double-circle earrings dominate.

They're echoed by a circular nose ring, a series of small circular earrings, and even by a series of modified circular acorn forms in the fabric of her dress and headdress.

Similarly, the repetition of circular forms unifies the outdoor setting, facing page, left, which reads almost as a performance of a circular dance troupe! The designer of the floral centerpiece selected crespidia, a spherical flower, and clustered most of them in a large vase filled with marbles to the left, echoed by a smaller cluster in a bud vase, right. These central elements relate strongly to the circular movements that form the chair backrests. Even the table that supports the floral arrangement is circular.

KENNETH TRUMBAUER, *Untitled,* 2002.
Floral arrangement; crespedia, vodka glasses,
marbles, vodka cooler. *Art direction by*
Dana Irwin. Photo by Sandra Stambaugh.

IRENE DEAN, *Barrette,* 1999.
1 x 3¾ inches (2.5 x 9.5 cm). Polymer
clay, mokume gane. *Photo by Evan Bracken.*

DANA IRWIN, *Blue Rooster Coaster,*
1999. 3 x 3 inches (7.5 x 7.5 cm).
Graphite.

Polymer clay artist Irene Dean uses repeating ovals to unify the
design of *Barrette*, top right. Here the oval appears in many
varieties: larger and smaller, circular and elongated, joined and
separate, fully intact and fragmentary. While almost all are light
yellow outlined in dark brown, a couple are black in the middle, providing a nice tension. And a secondary motif—that of
the five-point star—appears several times as a frame for the
oval. The surface design is unified while offering enough variation to keep the eye engaged. Likewise, Dana Irwin's restaurant logo, bottom right, uses repeating triangles and triangle
variations, with a secondary motif of circles.

JEAN WILLIAMS CACICEDO,
Lotus, 2000. 84 x 78 x ⅛ inches
(213.3 x 198.1 x .3 cm).
Woven wool and mohair; fulled,
clamp resist dyed, knit,
appliquéd, stitched, shibori.
Photo by Barry Shapiro.

ELIZABETH MURRAY, *Bowtie,*
2000. 85 x 77½ inches
(215.9 x 196.9 cm).
Oil on canvas.
Photo by Kerry R. McFate.
Courtesy of Pace Wildenstein
© *Elizabeth Murray.*

Variations of a modified circle—much like a pie missing a slice—repeat in Jean Williams Cacicedo's wearable art design *Lotus*, above. They appear prominently on the body and arms, and they hover underneath the top layers of fabric, providing an echo of the motif.

Contemporary painter Elizabeth Murray takes the idea of achieving unity through repetition of rounded forms to a most intricate and sophisticated extreme in *Bowtie*, above. The more you look, the more circular elements and

movements you'll find. Murray's design space consists of a series of canvases whose organic shapes twist, turn, and press against one another to form one large, round-edged underlying shape. This shape contains small circles, concentric circles, circles containing smaller circles each being pressed into ovals by larger forms on each side, and rounded bumps. Even the blue form at the bottom implies two connected ovals, as does the pink form inside.

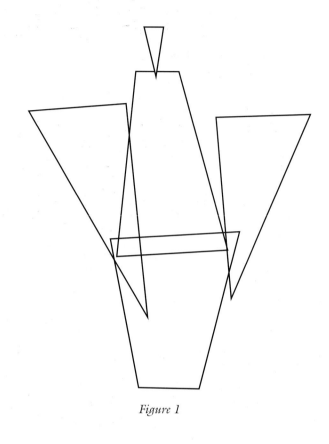

Figure 1

JOHN PRIP, *Silver Coffeepot,* 1958.
11¾ x 9¼ x 4½ inches
(29.8 x 23.5 x 11.4 cm).
Raised and fabricated silver
with ebony handle.
*Renwick Gallery, Washington, DC.
Smithsonian Museum,
Washington, DC/Art Resource, NY.*

John Prip uses the cone and its two-dimensional counterpart, the triangle, as the unifying shape motif in his silver and ebony *Silver Coffeepot,* above. The vessel's main body consists of two cones stacked together. The ebony knob on the lid stands as an inverted cone at the top, and the two very large and elegant negative spaces are triangular in character, providing beautiful responses to the positive form of the coffeepot (see figure 1).

The Limbourg Brothers' 15th-century manuscript illustration *May (Festival of May),* facing page, left, is an unusually rich and intricate composition in which the three primary colors each serve as repeating motifs that weave harmonious patterns through the space. Blue is the dominant motif. In spite of variations in scale and shape, repeated notes of deep, highly saturated blue lead the eye on a journey from left to right. At the same time, red repeats as a subordinate

motif in a way that's quite responsive and harmonious to the blues. Yellow repeats as a third color motif, while both black and white repeat themselves horizontally. And several shapes also repeat to form powerful rhythms: the pointed vertical roofs in the background, vertical tree trunks just below, and a series of modified circles in the horses in the foreground.

Finally, consider the simple color and shape motifs that work together in a surprisingly complex art deco poster, *Vichy (Demandez Votre Quart),* by Paul Colin, facing page, right. Warm mid-tone tan is the dominant motif; it repeats in an interesting variety of shapes that unify the space. Notice, however, how they establish a circular movement in the interior. The underlying forms in blue and white contain a number of circular shapes as secondary motifs that relate nicely to the circular movement in tan.

PAUL COLIN, *Vichy (Demandez Votre Quart),* c. 1940. 45 x 62 inches (114.3 x 157.5 cm). *Bibliothèque Nationale de France.*

LIMBOURG BROTHERS, *May (Festival of May),* 15th century. Calendar miniature from the Très Riches Heures du Duc de Berry. *Photo by R.G. Ojeda. Musée Condé, Chantilly, France. Réunion des Musées Nationaux/Art Resource, NY.*

■ EXERCISE 1

STAMPING TO INVESTIGATE REPETITION OF MOTIF

For this first challenge, we'll keep it simple: one shape only (to eliminate contrast of shape and scale) and one color only (to eliminate all color contrast except that of light and dark).

What You Need

Rubber stamp (one with a bold, simple design, such as a letter or number)

Rubber stamp pad (one color)

Several rectangular surfaces to stamp on, such as flat pieces of paper, cardboard, or mat board in a size of your choice.

What You Do

1. Load your stamp with ink, and press the stamp once anywhere on your surface. You have now established the presence of your motif in the space.

2. Without applying any more ink to the stamp, press it again and perhaps a third time anywhere on the surface. You'll notice that the motif begins to take on variety as it loses ink and becomes more faint. Artists who do monoprints call this kind of second stamping a "ghost."

3. Reink your stamp and, somewhere else in the space, press more firmly on one side of the stamp than on the other. This gives you another variation: the motif will be more solidly established on one of its sides than on the other.

4. Clean the excess ink from the stamp, then ink only the top portion of the stamp. You'll get yet another variation: the motif in partial or fragmented form.

5. Next, try stamping at the edge of your surface, allowing part of the motif to disappear completely off the edge. You'll get another instance of a partial motif.

6. Finally, stamp several times with full pressure and a fully inked stamp, allowing an instance or two where the stamped motifs overlap.

Analysis

By this point, you can see a number of principles at work in your design. The space is unified by the repetition of your motif. At the same time, there's plenty of variety in the space. The motif ranges from whole to fragmentary, is uniformly and non-uniformly stamped, and stands alone and is joined

together by overlapping. You also see the color contrast of value. The motif is darker where the stamping pressure was most firm and when the stamp was most fully inked. It's lighter where the stamping pressure was softer and where you "ghost stamped." Your design is further unified by the fully inked, evenly stamped forms that appear most often. And you've accomplished all this with little or no planning and by using just one shape and just one color.

Now, take out another stamping surface. Using the same single stamp and single color, repeat the exercise. Introduce the motif a few times, sense how the space feels, and try to determine what you might like to do next to the design in response. Continue the process until you've taken it as far as you'd like to go.

Variations

For the following variations, you'll need two or more additional rubber stamps with different shapes on them, and at least two more stamp pads featuring different ink colors.

Variation 1

Repeat Exercise 1, this time using more than one ink color. Establish a color organization (see the sections on color, beginning on page 66) as a secondary way to unify the space and to introduce more variety.

Variation 2

Repeat Exercise 1, sticking with one ink color, but this time using at least one additional stamp to introduce further variety in shape. Make sure the original shape still dominates enough to be the organizing motif. Use the additional shapes to add interest and tension to the design.

Variation 3

Repeat Exercise 1, using several different stamps and a number of ink colors at once. This time, allow color to be your motif, independent of shape. To do so, ink several different stamps with the same color, and use it as the unifying motif in the space. Ink the same stamps with a couple of other colors. Apply these colors as contrasts and variety in the design.

Variation 4

Repeat Exercise 1, this time using a three-dimensional object as your surface for shapes stamped in as many colors as you like. This object might be a large paper cup, an old book, a thrift-store lampshade, a white baseball cap—anything that strikes your fancy. The same principles hold true for this design, but you'll want to consider how satisfying your design is from several angles at once. You might even want to line up a series of cups, eggs, or other objects and decorate them all, responding to how the stamped images on the different forms speak to one another and to the spaces in between.

■ EXERCISE 2

COLLAGE

Now, apply repetition of motif in a medium that offers you more flexibility and variety: collage. If Rembrandt had had piles of *People* and *Good Housekeeping* stacked around the house, he undoubtedly would have created compositions in collage. But in the 17th century, paper was a rare and valuable commodity. Tearing it up and pasting it to something wasn't even considered. In our society, paper is everywhere, much of it considered throwaway junk. It's also ideal material with which to explore ideas and even create finished designs. Collage elements furnish you with an almost infinite range of shape, color, and texture.

What You Need

Magazines, newspapers, cloth samples, or any relatively
    flat material that you can easily cut or tear and paste
    to a surface

Scissors (optional)

Adhesive (Acrylic medium [flat, gloss, or gel] works.
    White craft glue is an inexpensive substitute.)

A surface to collage, either two dimensional or
    three dimensional (paper, cardboard, mat board, canvas,
    cloth, a large paper cup, an old book, an old lampshade,
    a baseball cap, etc.)

What You Do

1. Choose a motif, such as a shape or color, cut and/or tear a series of variations, and begin arranging them on your surface. Be aware of how the individual shapes begin to relate to each other in the space. Keep in mind that every square inch of your space takes part in your design.

2. Move the pieces around, then respond by adding, subtracting, and rearranging.

3. Remember, the repeating shape will unify your design, while any variations you introduce will create interest and tension.

4. Continue this process of responding to your evolving design until you've taken it as far as you wish.

CHAPTER 6

RHYTHM

You're probably quite familiar with the notion of rhythm; you experience it everyday, in the most fundamental ways. Your heartbeat, for example, repeats in a regular, orderly manner and establishes a rhythm that underlies your very existence. Breathing consists of a regular sequence of inhaling and exhaling. When you walk, you establish parallel rhythms with the two sides of your body.

Visual rhythm is created when elements repeat in a sequence in a design. The repeated elements are often shape or color motifs, such as the ones described in the last chapter. What's different here is that, rather than simply repeating, the elements create a pattern. They act as a series of beats that "speak" to one another. Variations in the character of the beats and in the relationships of the spaces between the

beats create the nature of the rhythm. Other times, the elements that establish rhythm vary in shape and color, and are tied together only in their role as rhythm makers.

Examples

To begin your exploration of designs organized around visual rhythm, look at *Honey Locust* by Michael Sherrill, facing page. This delicately balanced ceramic sculpture shows two strong sets of rhythmic relationships. The first is the orderly repetition of a double leaf motif at evenly spaced intervals along two stems. The design's primary variation occurs in the scale of these forms, which become progressively smaller as they move away from the base. The second rhythm is in the linear movement of the two stems. They take off from the primary branch at the base and create long, elegant, looping movements.

In contrast to Sherrill's open and lyrical rhythms, consider the compressed, staccato rhythms in the detail of an 11th-century Iranian Koran page, below, which shows embellished Arabic lettering. The primary rhythm of this rich piece is a series of vertical bars that move horizontally. They look like four trees, with a fifth that's been split and bent into an arrow shape, and a last, full tree on the far right. If you were listening to this rhythm, it would sound like this: one beat, a short rest, three quick beats, a long rest, a jarring variation of the earlier beats, and a loud firm closing beat.

MICHAEL SHERRILL, *Honey Locust,* 2001. 18 x 28 x 11 inches (45.7 x 71 x 27.9 cm). Porcelain. *Photo by Tim Barnwell.*

LEAF FROM THE KORAN (DETAIL), 11th century. 12⁷/₈ x 9 inches (32.7 x 22.7 cm). Black ink on light brown glazed paper. Rogers Fund, 1940 (40.164.2a). Photograph © The Metropolitan Museum of Art.

Toaster from Universal product line, 1918-1923. Manufactured by Landers, Frary & Clark, New Britain, CT. *Collection of Carole and Larry Meeker.*

JEAN HICKS, *Black Ziggurat,* 2000. 18 x 8 inches diam. (46 x 20.5 cm). Hand-felted, hand-blocked merino wool. Modeled by the artist. *Photo by Jan Cook. Courtesy www.jeanhicks.com.*

LEE SIPE, *Mended Wave,* 1995. 15 x 19 inches (38.1 x 48.3 cm). Pine needles, raffia, clay. *Photo by Evan Bracken.*

Vertical bars form a secondary rhythmic sequence on the lower front face of a vintage toaster, direction, a model manufactured by Landers, Frary & Clark from 1918 through 1923. The sequence runs parallel to and in support of the dominant rhythm, the series of toast-holders that loop their way across the top. The middle note of this seven-loop sequence features an additional loop at its apex, acting as both an accent note and a handle.

A cluster of modified cylinders, stacked one on another, creates the bold rhythmic movement that forms Jean Hicks's *Ziggurat*, facing page, right. The movement is capped by a cone, an exciting end to the sequence.

The shiny glass lollipops contrasting with the sandblasted hands in *Menorah with Lollipops and Hands* by Elizabeth Ryland Mears, top right, establish a strong, simple rhythm: DULL, shiny, shiny, shiny, DULL, shiny, shiny, shiny, DULL.

Choker #86 by Mary Lee Hu, bottom right, exhibits an especially graceful series of rhythms designed to be decorative. The repeated movement here is elegantly rounded and looping. The rhythmic repetition of the loop motif varies subtly from the right side to the left. The movement on the right begins with a long, open movement, then becomes increasingly compressed. The movement on the left is very moderately compressed all along the sequence.

Lee Sipe's *Mended Wave*, facing page, bottom, is another example of a simple looping movement acting as a repeated rhythmic element. Its major rhythm consists of the series of large, rounded forms that protrude at the middle of the vessel. A second series emerges below. The edges at the vessel opening create a third looping rhythm. Its interior is supported by two additional rhythmic sequences in the top half of the basket: parallel linear movements in the pine needles themselves, and a counter series of parallel movements in the basket's stitching.

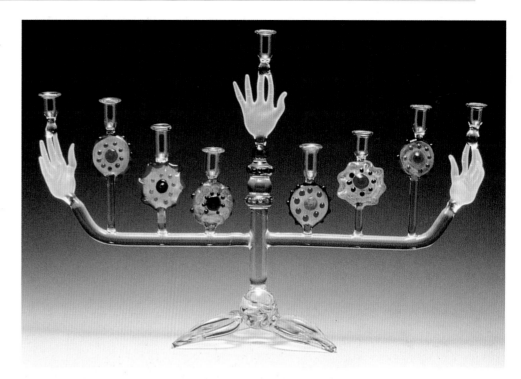

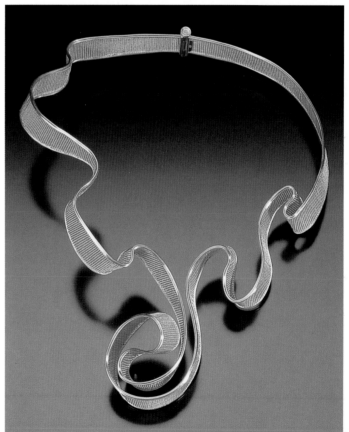

ELIZABETH RYLAND MEARS, *Menorah with Lollipops and Hands,* 1994.
17½ x 16½ x 8 inches (44.5 x 41.9 x 20.3 cm).
Flameworked and sandblasted glass. *Photo by John Russell.*

MARY LEE HU, *Choker #86,* 2000.
8 x 6½ x 1½ inches (20.3 x 16.5 x 3.8 cm).
Twined and fabricated 18 and 22 karat gold.
Photo by Doug Yaple.

In *Group Deciding*, top left, Jan Ternent uses rhythmic spacing in an exciting manner. Formally, her composition reads, from left to right: a compressed cluster of vertical, figurative notes; an empty space to pause; another compressed cluster; a second open interval; and, finally, a single figurative note. Think of this rhythmic spacing as breathing: in-out, in-out, in. Ternent's spacing also helps tell the story: two groups facing one another and sharing opinions while one lone figure stands apart.

In *East Lambrook Garden,* bottom left, Charles Mann creates a visual rhythm meant to be walked right into and experienced. On each side of this walkway is a row of evergreens that have been sculpted into a series of round forms that read as individual beats. The sequence is unified by the similarity of the beats and by their fairly uniform spacing. Variety and tension occur in a number of ways. Each of the evergreens leans, twists, and bends in a slightly different fashion, establishing a slightly different character to its beat. They also recede in space and turn with the curve in the pathway, so the round motif becomes fragmentary. The elements *between* the evergreen forms, such as the red flowers, are part of the rhythm as well. In this case, the repeating reds form the nice surprise of a minor counter-rhythm.

An exquisite example of 20th-century African-American quiltmaking, *Green Snake Quilt* by Susie Ponds, facing page, again features a series of parallel beats, this time formed by wavelike linear elements. At first glance, this composition seems simple and straightforward: wavy lines of nearly identical width, waving in a very similar fashion at very regular intervals. So why is it so lively and animated? For starters, Ponds's wavy lines are not really that similar at all. There are slight modulations throughout. Also the colors contrast differently with the different-colored squares of fabric "underneath," creating a rhythm that is surprisingly rich and varied.

JAN TERNENT, *Group Deciding,* 2000. 48 x 36 inches (121.9 x 91.4 cm). Oil. *Photo by artist.*

CHARLES MANN, *East Lambrook Garden,* 1991. Color photograph of a garden in Wiltshire, England. Garden designer: Marjorie Fish.

SUSIE PONDS, *Green Snake Quilt,* 1979. 64 x 80 inches (162.6 x 203.2 cm). Quilted. *From the collection of Maude and James Wahlman. Originally published in Wahlman,* Signs and Symbols.

Kuo Hsi, *Clearing Autumn Skies Over Mountains and Valleys,* 81 1/8 x 10 1/4 inches (206 x 25.7 cm). Ink and tint on silk. *Freer Gallery of Art, Washington DC.*

Several parallel rhythms move from left to right in Kuo Hsi's *Clearing Autumn Skies Over Mountains and Valleys*, all very elegant and featuring subtle contrasts. They also delicately connect with one another, contributing to a feeling of unity and wholeness. One sequence runs through the mountain peaks at the top of the space. The repeated shape here is a rounded top, and the nature of the beats varies beautifully, from hard edged to softer, quite dark to faint, and strong clusters to isolated peaks. A second sequence is formed by the spider-like rounded tops of the trees that run from just left of middle in a horizontal fashion to the right.

Exercises

■ EXERCISE 1

USING VISUAL CONTRAST AS RHYTHM

Let's really isolate how rhythm works by eliminating all visual contrasts except for one: contrast of value. In this exercise, you'll work with no contrast of shape, scale, texture, mark, or hue, and very little variation in placement and orientation. With all of those elements eliminated from a design, can you still establish an interesting rhythm? You bet.

What You Need

Ruler

Pencil

White or midtone neutral-color flat surface, such as paper, cardboard, or mat board in a size of your choice (minimum, 8 1/2 x 11 inches [21.6 x 27.9 cm])

Graphite or charcoal pencil (If you have black and white paints still on hand from the color exercises, you can mix grays and do this challenge in paint, if you like.)

Pencil sharpener for graphite or eyebrow pencil sharpener for charcoal

Kneaded eraser (optional)

What You Do

1. With the ruler and pencil, lightly mark off a horizontal row of 18 vertical bars, each 2 inches (5.1 cm) tall by 3/8 inch (9.5 mm) wide (see figure 1).

2. Limiting yourself to three to five tones from the value scale (see page 68), fill in the vertical bars, repeating the tones at intervals to establish a rhythmic sequence (see figure 2 as an example).

Remember to fill in the bars in a consistent fashion, nice and smooth or with consistency of mark. This will ensure that contrasts of mark and of activity versus passivity won't interfere with your experience of value alone as rhythm maker.

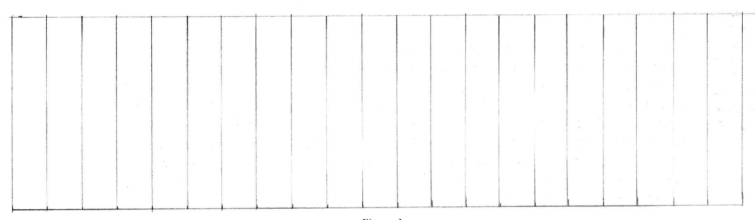

Figure 1

Figure 2

▪ EXERCISE 2

CONTRAST OF SCALE AS RHYTHM MAKER

This time, try using contrast of scale (changes in size or area covered) as the way to establish rhythm.

What You Need

Ruler

Pencil

White or midtone neutral-color flat surface, such as paper, cardboard, or mat board in a size of your choice (minimum, 8-1/2 x 11 inches [21.6 x 27.9 cm])

Graphite or charcoal pencil (substitute black paint or pastel pencil, if you prefer)

Pencil sharpener for graphite or eyebrow pencil sharpener for charcoal

What You Do

1. With the ruler and pencil, lightly mark off a long horizontal band or rectangle, 2 inches (5.1 cm) tall by a minimum of 8 inches (20.3 cm) long, longer if you prefer.

2. Using black only, begin filling in the horizontal space with vertical bars that stay within the horizontal space at the top and bottom, but vary from thick to thin. Repeat these different-sized bars at intervals to establish a rhythmic sequence.

Notice how, just as the black vertical bars establish a sequence of beats, so do the white bars that serve as the intervals between the black bars. You can take it even further and read the white bars as the beats, with the black bars serving as the series of intervals in between. In fact, you could just as well have done this exercise with white on a black surface.

▪ EXERCISE 3

STAMPING TO EXPLORE RHYTHMIC REPETITION OF SHAPE

Now, try relying on the repetition of a shape motif to establish a feeling of rhythm. You'll want to work with variations in placement and orientation of the shape to get the results you're after.

What You Need

Pencil

Ruler

Several flat rectangular surfaces, such as pieces of paper, cardboard, or mat board in sizes of your choice

Rubber stamp (one with a bold, simple design, such as a letter or number)

Rubber stamp pad (one color)

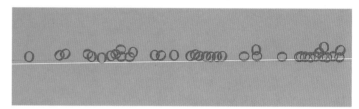

Figure 3

What You Do

1. With the pencil and ruler, mark off a very light horizontal line from one edge of one of the surfaces all the way to the other.

2. Ink the stamp fully with one color, and begin stamping your shape motif in the space in a variety of ways, all of which touch the horizontal line somehow (see figure 3). Fully ink the stamp and press firmly each time, to eliminate changes in the nature of the shape itself. However, do vary its placement, so it's higher or lower, leaning to the left or right, turned on its side, or upside down. You might also try varying the intervals between the appearances of the shape. Some shapes may overlap, others might stand in a close cluster, and others might be spaced far apart. The only structure is that all the shapes will appear in a linear sequence.

3. Now, on another surface, place and orient the stamped shape so it creates a pattern that is a rhythm (see figure 4). The possibilities here are abundant—an interesting fact, considering that you're using one shape and one color in a narrowly structured framework.

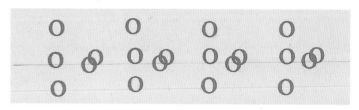

Figure 4

Variation

The earlier exercises address rhythm as it occurs in a linear sequence, from left to right. This format occurs often in designs, and it offers a clear and simple structure for exploration. For variation, repeat Exercise 3, this time replacing the horizontal line with a large, looping figure eight that engulfs much of your surface. Mark the figure eight with a pencil, and begin stamping the same way you did above, this time making sure that all the stamp motifs touch the figure eight line in some way. Again, repeat placement and orientation of the stamp motif in ways that establish a strong visual rhythm (see figure 5).

Figure 5

■ EXERCISE 4

USING COLLAGE TO ESTABLISH RHYTHMIC REPETITION OF COLOR

Here's your chance to do two pretty wonderful things at once. One, you'll be designing in collage, free from most of the structures imposed by the last few challenges. And two, you can explore creating rhythm with color.

What You Need

Magazines, newspapers, cloth samples, or any relatively flat material that you can easily cut or tear and paste to a surface

Scissors (optional)

Adhesive (Acrylic medium [flat, gloss, or gel] works. White craft glue is an inexpensive substitute.)

A surface to collage, either two dimensional or three dimensional (paper, cardboard, mat board, canvas, cloth, a large paper cup, an old book, an old lampshade, a baseball cap, etc.)

What You Do

1. Cut and tear a series of interesting shapes, and begin arranging them on your surface. You can repeat some shapes and shape variations, but don't rely on any one shape to be dominant as an organizing motif. Instead, you want to make a color act as a dominant motif, even though instances of that color will not have shape in common (see figure 6). You can decide on the color you'll use as your motif in advance, or you can let it emerge as you move pieces around and respond by adding, subtracting, and rearranging others.

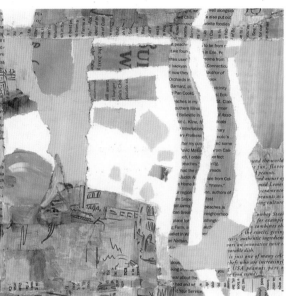

Figure 6

2. Notice how the individual shapes and colors begin to relate to each other in the space. Look for or establish recurrences of the color that begin to establish a rhythmic pattern, and respond. Keep in mind that every square inch of your space takes part in your design.

3. Continue this process of responding to your evolving design until it feels unified by a rhythmic movement established by color.

Additional Variations

You can repeat Exercises 1 through 4 a number of times each, exploring and establishing different rhythmic sequences each time. The more you experience establishing different rhythms in different ways, the more the idea of rhythm will become a part of your design vocabulary.

CHAPTER 7

SYMMETRICAL ARRANGEMENTS

Both symmetrical arrangements, the focus of this chapter,
and asymmetrical arrangements, discussed in the next one,
are based on balance.

BALANCE

A design is said to be balanced when elements are arranged
in a way that establishes a feeling of equilibrium. The design
seems settled, in place, or on an even keel. It doesn't lean to
one side or feel top or bottom heavy. An empty design space
is perfectly balanced. As soon as you introduce a visual element, even something as minimal as a black dot, tension
results, and the feeling of balance is in jeopardy. The space
is likely to lean, push, or pull to one side or to the top. And

as you introduce more elements, the
sense of balance is likely to vacillate
between states of relative equilibrium
and nonequilibrium. Your job, if you want
a balanced design, is to reestablish
equilibrium.

The process is very much like the physical challenge of balance. Try walking on a curb to
reacquaint yourself with it. Before long, you'll
probably feel as if you're leaning to one side or
the other. Reflexively, you'll attempt to compensate. If your left shoulder drops and your body
starts falling to the left, you'll extend your right arm
to the side and elevate it to stop your fall. If you
compensate too much, you might start to fall
right, instead, in which case you'll compensate
again. Throughout your walk you'll continue to
make adjustments. This is the same sort of intuitive sensing that goes into the design process.

You can also think of balancing elements in another
way. Imagine an old-fashioned scale, with one side connected by a cord to the end of a second scale. Imagine
that this second scale is connected by a cord of a different length to a third scale, and so on until you have a
room full of scales, all connected by different lengths of
cord. If you place a weight on one side of one of the
scales, the entire system of scales bobs up and down.
To reestablish equilibrium, you'd need to start adding
weights elsewhere, moving them around, and perhaps
removing others until you got things back to level.
Again, think of designing as this kind of process, where
weights are introduced, juggled, moved, removed, and
reintroduced in a variety of arrangements until you
achieve a balanced resolution.

Symmetry is one of two primary forms of balance. It occurs when elements on one side of a composition are mirrored by like elements on the opposite side or when elements are mirrored top to bottom. Such arrangements are inherently balanced. Symmetrical balance is easy to understand, because it comes naturally. The human body itself is symmetrical, so we're very familiar with the concept. Our bodies have a central axis along which key elements such as the nose and navel are located and from which everything radiates. And whenever we have a feature off to one side of this axis (an eye or elbow, for example), it's mirrored by a similar feature on the other side.

Symmetrical balance is also relatively easy to achieve. All you have to do is establish a central axis in the middle of a space, place any elements you want on the axis, place other elements to one side of the axis, repeat those elements in mirrored placement on the other side, and you've got it. You can continue to add, modify, and subtract elements, as long as you make corresponding modifications on the opposite side.

Perfect symmetry, symmetrical balance with no variation at all, produces a rock-solid arrangement (see figure 1). Everything is in order and stable, and the configuration is firm and static. This type of balance is easily understood and quite predictable, and it's perfectly suited to a number of decorative and narrative design purposes. On the other hand, because this kind of symmetry results in unity without variety, it often lacks the visual tension, complexity, and intrigue necessary for other design purposes, such as evoking strong mood or creating exciting movement.

Modified symmetry, symmetrical balance with subtle variations, can produce enormously satisfying tensions while retaining a sense of solidity and unity (see figure 2). Modified symmetry results when mirrored elements are tweaked or altered and then responded to. Take a design featuring a vertical bar in the middle of a space, several identical circles stacked evenly on the bar, and a column of evenly spaced identical squares mirroring each other on the left and right of the bar. Say you shifted the top circle ever so slightly to the right side of the bar. While the arrangement would remain essentially symmetrical, you'd begin to experience the design as leaning slightly to the right. Then, perhaps you'd make the top square on the left stack slightly darker than the rest of the

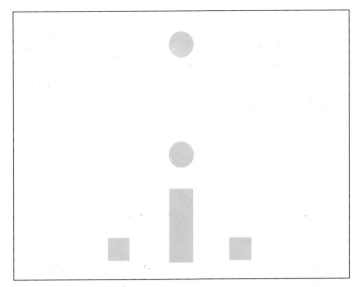

Figure 1

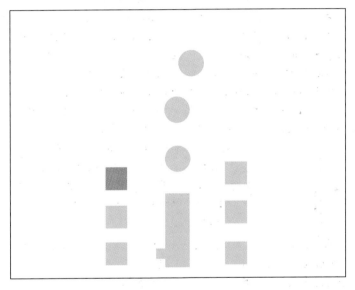

Figure 2

squares. This would visually push everything back to the left and nearer to balance. If you still experienced the design as leaning ever so slightly to the right or feeling too top heavy, you might put a little "bump" on the left edge of the central bar, near the bottom, to reestablish equilibrium. The design would now be balanced according to modified symmetry, or symmetry with a series of subtle variations. You could keep introducing more mirrored elements and modifying them, performing the kind of juggling act referred to earlier. Just be aware that if you press the tweaking process to the point where the symmetry is just barely operative, the design may be more asymmetrical, which we'll discuss in detail in the next chapter.

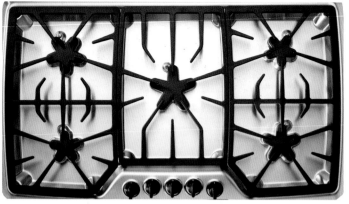

Examples

Consider the functional metal design *Portal Gates,* left, executed by Albert Raymond Paley as a commission for the Renwick Gallery in Washington, D.C. This arrangement exhibits nearly perfect symmetry. Each element on one side is mirrored by an identical element in identical placement on the other. This side-to-side mirroring is often referred to as bilateral symmetry. The one exception is the handle, on the right edge of the left door panel. You might think Paley introduced one handle simply to satisfy the utilitarian need for a way to open the gate. But he could have added a second handle, whether functional or not, on the right door. It seems that Paley liked having one element that didn't quite fit the system.

Symmetry is also at work in the sculptural design of this stove top by Bosch Corporation, above. Its perfect bilateral symmetry even includes five dark heat adjustment knobs, one on the central axis, and two on each side.

Bilateral symmetry can exist in a top-to-bottom arrangement as well, as is the case in Lee Dunkel's black-and-white documentary photograph *Shell Creek*, facing page. Dunkel takes advantage of the reflective mirroring found in nature. The horizon line provides the design's central axis, from which the thickest and heaviest linear movements in the fallen tree loop down to form powerful, compelling shapes. The shapes mirror one another above and below the axis. The design's symmetry is modified somewhat. The bottom of the space is a bit darker and denser, and it includes a bit of foreground shoreline, which reinforces the tranquility of the space.

ALBERT RAYMOND PALEY, *Portal Gates,* 1974. 90¾ x 72 x 4 inches (230.5 x 182.9 x 10.2 cm). Forged steel, brass, copper, and bronze. *Commissioned for the Renwick Gallery. Smithsonian American Art Museum, Washington, DC/Art Resource, NY.*

Stovetop. *Photo courtesy of the Thermador Corporation.*

LEE DUNKEL, *Shell Creek,* 1995. 15 x 15 inches (38.1 x 38.1 cm). Black and white silver print. *Collection of the artist.*

MARY S. PARKER, *Syrian Dress Yoke with Machine Embroidery,* 2001. 25 x 25 inches (63.5 x 63.5 cm). Rayon embroidery thread on cotton lawn, inspired by Syrian garment owned by Alexandra Hart. *Photo by Evan Bracken.*

This beautiful Syrian dress yoke by Mary S. Parker, facing page, features mirrored elements along more than one axis simultaneously. When this sort of symmetry is used consistently throughout a design, the result is radial symmetry (see Linda Arndt's *Kaleidescope for David*, page 97, as an example). In this case, the radial symmetry is tweaked by differences in the top triangle and in the lower quadrant.

Wayne Thiebaud's painting *Around the Cake*, top right, is a good example of modified radial symmetry. Spin the image around, and you'll see a mirroring of elements no matter what your vantage point. Thiebaud achieves a rock-solid arrangement this way, then tweaks the elements to achieve subtle tension. We see two sides on some cake slices, three on others, as well as differing orientations, shapes, colors, and sizes.

At first glance, Renie Breskin Adams's embroidery composition *Hands Like Wings*, bottom right, appears to be symmetrically structured. After all, it features the shapes of a table and a blue sky background centered on a middle axis, a flying human figure in the center of the sky, three birds on each side in the sky, six cup and saucer sets arranged in three rows of two on each side, and tall purple rectangles overlapped by figures on each side at the outside edges.

Perfect symmetry, right? Not so fast. Notice the numerous ways Adams throws this apparent mirroring out of whack. The three birds in the sky on each side aren't mirrored at all. They differ in shape, size, color, and placement. Same story with the coffee cups and with the three birds on and in the cups. Finally, though the mind registers a figure on each side at the outside edge, the eye notices that the shape and color of the figures' garments are very different, and that the chair on the left has much more presence than the one on the right. Taken as a whole, however, the feeling of symmetry is clearly present. The many instances where elements or attributes don't quite fit give the design its liveliness.

WAYNE THIEBAUD, *Around the Cake,* 1962. 22 x 28 inches (55.9 x 71.1 cm). Oil on canvas. *Spencer Museum of Art: The University of Kansas, Lawrence, KS. Gift of Ralph T. Coe in memory of Helen F. Spencer.*

RENIE BRESKIN ADAMS, *Hands Like Wings,* 1996. 5 5/8 x 6 inches (14.3 x 15.2 cm). Hand embroidered cotton. *Photo by artist. Private collection.*

"Hands Like Wings"   Renie

JOHN WHIPPLE,
Journal, 2000.
32 x 40 inches
(81.3 x 101.6 cm).
Charcoal on birch; sealed
and coated with layers of
translucent oil glazes.
Photo by Randall Smith.

Figure 1

John Whipple's oil painting *Journal,* left, is another interesting and informative example of modified symmetry. Not a single element is placed squarely on a central axis. Although there are similar elements from side to side, none mirror exactly. So how and why does this composition work, and what holds it together? As you can see in figure 1, Whipple establishes a clear feeling of symmetry by *nearly* mirroring shapes that are exceedingly powerful. These elements command our attention and establish a quasi-symmetrical framework that's solid. The symmetrical nature of Whipple's design is reinforced by the large, black, hard-edged shape of the torso, shoulders, and neck, which is nearly centered and serves as a grounding element at the bottom.

Albert Cheuret's design of the art deco clock, facing page, bottom, feels very stable, again due to its nearly perfect bilateral symmetry, not to mention the repetition of a triangle motif found nearly throughout. What's the element that doesn't fit into perfect symmetry here? The clock's hands, one longer than the other, of course!

The Colander/Fool: Card # 0 in the Kitchen Tarot, by Susan Shie and James Acord, facing page, top left, is a jazzy composition full of vibrating rhythms, the complete range of color the wheel has to offer, narrative text, and figurative forms that come together around a colander as body. And what holds all these lively and disparate elements together? A strong sense of modified bilateral symmetry.

Finally, consider the extraordinarily strong, intuitive sense of symmetry exhibited in eight-year-old Lucy Ballentine's *Fishing,* facing page, top right. There's a clear central axis, ever so slightly to the left of center. Located right on it is a blue fish at the end of a fishing line (the focus of the visual "story" Ballentine is telling), a blue-green wavy weed, and a dark "V" shape at the bottom. Mirrored on each side are waves, two pale purple fish, two wavy reeds, and rounded mounds of sea floor.

Ballentine's real genius comes out in her tweaking of the symmetry. First, she pulls your eye sharply to the top left with the warm, red-orange fisherman and boat. To counter this, the purple fish on the right is higher than the one on the left, pulling the eye to the right. Then, a red creature pulls you all

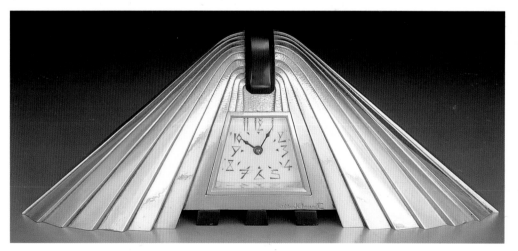

SUSAN SHIE AND JAMES ACORD, *The Colander/Fool: Card # O in the Kitchen Tarot,* 1998. 34 x 20 inches (86.4 x 50.8 cm). Hand appliqué, quilting, embellishing (Lucky School of Quilting Techniques). *Photo by Susan Shie.*

LUCY BALLENTINE, *Fishing,* 2002. 8½ x 11 inches (21.6 x 27.9 cm). Metallic ink on paper. *Photo by keithwright.com. Courtesy of the artist.*

ALBERT CHEURET, *Clock,* c. 1930. 6¼ x 16½ x 4 inches (15.9 x 41.9 x 10.1 cm). Silvered bronze, onyx. *Photo by Katherine Wetzel. Virginia Museum of Fine Arts, Richmond, VA. Gift of Sydney and Frances Lewis. © Virginia Museum of Fine Arts.*

the way off the right edge, at the top of one mound of sea floor, which is also higher and larger on the right. This visual weight, in turn, is countered by a pink starfish that pulls to the lower left. Finally, a little gray note pulls us to the lower left edge. Ballentine's design encourages viewers to move all around the space in a satisfying way, but our experience is unified by a symmetry that remains strongly intact.

Exercises

■ EXERCISE 1

STAMPING TO EXPLORE PERFECT AND MODIFIED SYMMETRY

In this exercise, you'll create two related compositions. One demonstrates perfect symmetry. The other is a modified counterpart that incorporates a number of variations and responses.

What You Need

Pencil

Ruler

2 rectangular surfaces, such as flat pieces of paper, cardboard, or mat board in sizes of your choice

Several rubber stamps

Several rubber stamp pads (as many colors as you like)

What You Do

1. On both surfaces, use the pencil and ruler to mark off a vertical center line that cuts the rectangular space in half from left to right.

2. On one surface, begin a design by placing stamped shapes either right on the centerline or to one side of the

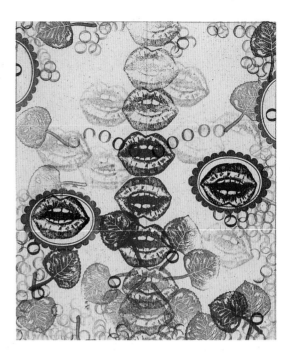

line. Anytime you place a shape on one side or the other, mirror it exactly on the opposite side.

3. Continue stamping until you're satisfied with the arrangement. You now have a space that is balanced according to perfect symmetry. Easy, yes?

4. Now comes the more complex and creative part. On your second surface, begin a second design by placing some similar elements in placements similar to those in the first design. This time, however, disrupt or tweak the symmetry just a bit. For example, you might raise or lower an element, make one tilt in a different direction, and so on.

5. As you continue to add stamped elements similar to those in the first design, respond to your initial modifications with others in an attempt to reestablish equilibrium. Continue, adding some new stamped images or eliminating others, until you're satisfied that the arrangement is both intriguing and strongly unified by a modified symmetry.

6. Compare the two arrangements. Which one is more stable and soothing, and which is more exciting and intriguing? What are the differences in the moods of the two pieces, and what causes the differences?

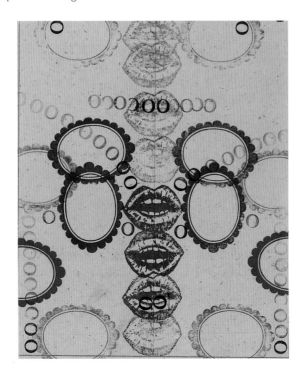

■ EXERCISE 2

COLLAGE COMPOSITION IN MODIFIED SYMMETRY

Now you'll be creating a design that can look any way you like, as long as it's unified according to modified symmetry. Working in collage gives you quick and easy access to a full range of shape, color, texture, line, and mark.

What You Need

Collage materials (magazines, newspapers, cloth samples, or any relatively flat material you can easily cut or tear and paste to a surface)

Scissors (optional)

Adhesive (Acrylic medium [flat, gloss, or gel] works well. White craft glue is an inexpensive substitute. You can also assemble this collage using any alternative technique you prefer, such as sewing pieces of fabric to a surface.)

A two-dimensional surface, such as paper, cardboard, mat board, canvas, or cloth

What You Do

1. You can begin and carry out this process any way you want. Start with a plan and stick to it. Use a plan as a way to get going, but be open to changing the plan or abandoning it altogether. Or, start without any preconceived notions at all; simply begin setting visual elements in place and then respond to them.

2. Begin, again, by placing some similar elements in symmetrical arrangements, then disrupt or tweak the symmetry a bit. As you do, take advantage of some of the distinct qualities that collage offers. Vary shapes by ripping some and cutting others, for example. In addition to adding pieces to the surface, pull some off now and then. Try to sense which elements the surface will let you have and which it insists on keeping.

3. Continue the process as long as you like. Add, alter, move, veil, obliterate and so on, as long as symmetry serves as the strong, unifying presence when you're finished.

CHAPTER 8

ASYMMETRICAL ARRANGEMENTS

Like the preceding chapter, this one considers the idea of balancing a design, this time using *asymmetry*. Generally, asymmetrical balance evokes a mood full of tension; its structure is inherently dynamic. Asymmetry involves ordering a design so it contains a variety of elements in varying and contrasting placements that still work together to establish equilibrium. This kind of arrangement achieves balance without the benefit of a central axis or mirrored elements. While symmetry establishes unity first and variety second (if at all), asymmetry features variety first and attempts to establish unity and balance in the process. Asymmetrical balance is typically created in one of the following two ways:

1. Different elements in different arrangements produce equivalent forces that offset one another. Take the analogy of the single scale with weights once again. In a symmetrical configuration, a weight would be placed on one side of the scale and an identical or very similar weight would be placed on the other, and the scale would even out in an easily understood manner. In an asymmetrical design, one large weight might be placed on one side of the scale, while several small and differently shaped weights that together equal the weight of the large one might be placed on the other side. The two sides would balance each other perfectly.

Or, think about riding a seesaw when you were a kid. If the person on the other side weighed a bit more than you did and sat in the middle of his or her seat, you had to lean waaaay back on your seat to get your side to drop down. Or, you might have moved much farther up the seat (toward the center fulcrum) to get your side to rise up. Back then, you knew intuitively that you could change the balance by changing the placement of your body on your seat. Now, take this idea and apply it to a visual design.

In these examples, the designs are balanced by juggling one area of the space against the other. There's still an implied axis or division of the space, though it's not necessarily in the middle.

2. Different elements in different combinations and arrangements act together in just the right combination to establish an overall feeling of balance.

Consider once again the room full of interconnected scales onto which you randomly place a number of different weights (page 122). All the scales in the room (not just the ones with weights) would shift up or down. To bring the whole system back into equilibrium, you'd need to add more weights here and subtract others there. A designer can bring a composition into asymmetrical balance in the same way, by juggling weights all over the space, playing one push against another pull, until the space feels balanced.

Examples

Albert Pinkham Ryder's *In the Stable*, facing page, top, is a textbook illustration of asymmetrical balance at work. Virtually all the powerful forces appear on the right side of the design. They include the largest shape (the white horse), which also represents the greatest value contrast in relation to the surrounding dark ground; the red garment, which stands as the purest and warmest color in the composition; and the rhythmic sequence of the little light chicks, which runs across the bottom right. So what balances the clustering of all these strong elements? Amazingly and unexpectedly, the little window at the left edge near the top does the job. How in the world does such an apparently small force act with enough weight to counter all those big weights on the other side?

For starters, elements placed in the upper left area of a design space garner greater attention than any others. Second, the window is very light in value, so it's in great contrast to the surrounding dark ground. Third, any visual activity reads with more force when it's placed in quiet,

ALBERT PINKHAM RYDER,
In The Stable, before 1911. 21 x 32 inches (53.4 x 81.3 cm). Oil on canvas mounted on fiberboard. *Smithsonian American Art Museum, Washington, DC/Art Resource, NY.*

passive surroundings, creating a contrast of activity/passivity. Finally, notice how the window shape is "crossed" by a vertical bar of a beam in the stable? This bar is part of an underlying rhythm of verticals that runs horizontally through the space. The window shape is the only prominent "punctuation" note on this sequence, which draws still further attention to it.

Gus Riley's *Plum Tomatoes and Green Cloth*, right, is quite similar to Ryder's painting. The most powerful and active area in the composition lies in the cluster of red plum tomatoes.

It represents the warmest set of elements; it stands strong because of its contrast of temperature. The largest element in the painting is the green cloth. It stands out because of the large area it covers, and because its green color forms a complementary contrast with the red. Again, everything in the

GUS RILEY,
Plum Tomatoes and Green Cloth, 1997. 8 x 10 inches (20.3 x 25.4 cm). Oil on board. *Photo by Beach Photo.*

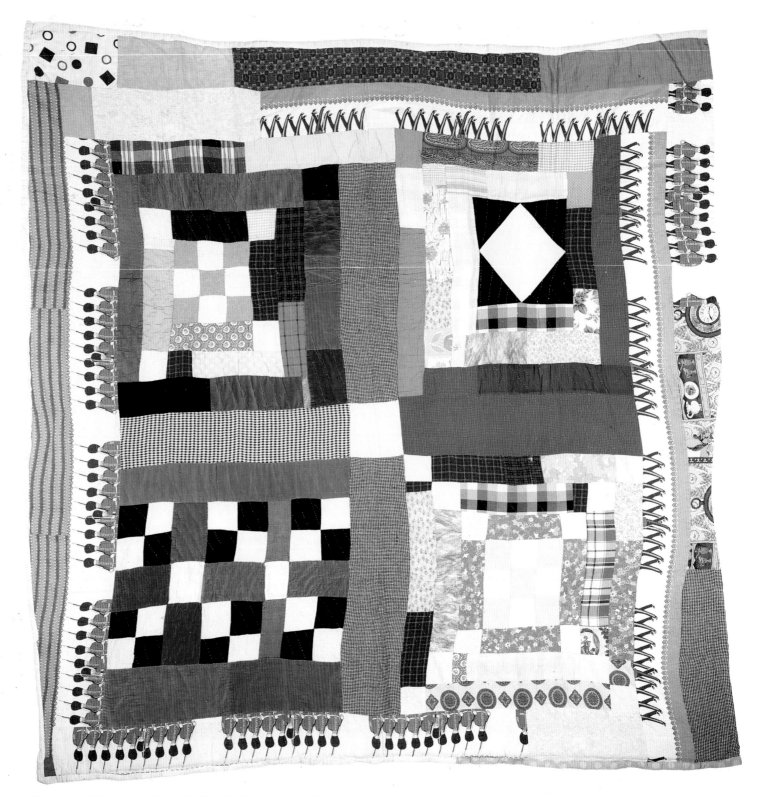

PLUMMER T. PETTWAY, *Block Quilt,* 1979. 66 x 80 inches (167.6 x 203.2 cm). Quilted.

From the collection of Maude and James Wahlman. Originally published in Wahlman, Signs and Symbols.

painting seems to want to move us to the right and lower areas of the space. So, what counters this and pushes us back to the left to help establish balance? Riley's equivalent of Ryder's little window is the pressure exerted on the space by the lines between the tiles and by the pointed edge of the green cloth, upper left. The linear movements of the lines cross the space and touch the outside edge in several places, encouraging the eye to experience the entire space. The most prominent of these movements is the one spot where the lines intersect (upper left, just above the green). Here, the folds crisscross to indicate "X marks the spot," or "look here." The effect is surprisingly powerful. Notice, too, how the pointed end of the green cloth acts as a little arrowhead. It also shouts "look this way." This movement is enhanced by Riley's thickening of the dark shadow just to the left of the point.

Block Quilt by Plummer T. Pettway, facing page, is based on a vaguely symmetrical grid of four near squares, two stacked above the other two. But the symmetry is tweaked so powerfully by so many relationships that the design has a strong asymmetrical arrangement. Each of the four square sections contains very different elements and forces. The most powerful is the one on the upper right, which contains a hard-edged white diamond shape surrounded by black. It's one of the few aspects of the design that presents diagonals, and it's the most powerful. It draws your eye up and right. The two squares stacked on the left are next in the power hierarchy, pulling us to the left. The bottom of the two has the most tension by virtue of its checkerboard pattern, featuring extreme light-dark contrast.

So, having orchestrated the eye to the upper right, and then to the bottom left, what does Pettway do to balance the arrangement? She places a white rectangle containing black-and-white circles and squares in the very upper left corner. This is where the eye goes as it begins to read a page, making the placement very powerful. Also, in the context of the long passages that make up the top and left side borders, this rectangle with squares and circles is by far the most highly activated, so it demands our attention.

The glazed earthenware design *Gas Can*, by Rick Dillingham, right, is another example of asymmetry at work.

RICK DILLINGHAM, *Gas Can,* 1981. 19 x 17¼ x 3⁷⁄₁₆ inches (48.3 x 43.8 x 8.9 cm). Glazed earthenware. *Gift of Mr. and Mrs. Joseph Luria and Trudy Luria Fisher from the collection of, and in memory of, Michael Stephen Luria. Smithsonian American Art Museum, Washington, DC/Art Resource, NY.*

2 *To keep the arrangement from feeling top and right-side heavy, linear movements converge here, while the spout breaks up the flowing lines. This draws attention away from the large form on the right and brings the design into balance.*

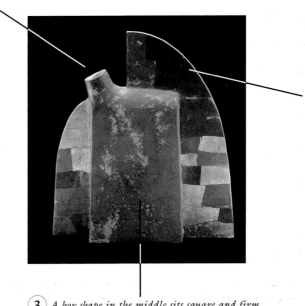

1 *The largest form lifts the eye toward the top and to the right.*

3 *A box shape in the middle sits square and firm.*

LYNN WHIPPLE, *Full Circle,* 2001. 32 x 40 inches (81.3 x 101.6 cm). Collage, acrylic, pencil on paper.
Photo by Randall Smith.

OLIVIER ROLLIN, *Hommage à Coco Channel,* 1998. Approximately 30 inches (76.2 cm) tall. Mixed media lamp.
Photo by Richard Babb.

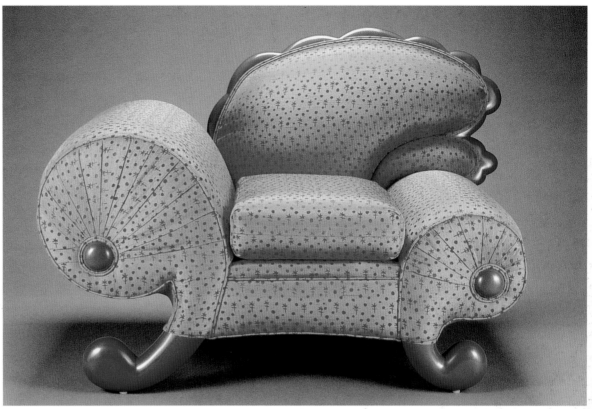

In *Full Circle*, facing page, right, Lynn Whipple uses two subtle compressions of space to balance an otherwise unbalanced arrangement. First, the figure of the woman sets the design into motion as it tilts to the left. Next, her arm on the right dissipates at the elbow. Whipple completes this counter movement to the right with the little finger-like dashes on the right edge of the oval, which is slightly off center to the right. This makes for a slight feeling of congestion on the right side. And how is this countered? The gray horizon line is angled ever so slightly higher on the left. It's supported by a red triangle at the bottom left corner, which is slightly larger than its counterpart on the right. These forces push slightly upward, compressing the white space above and making it feel smaller and more equal to the narrower white space on the right.

Richard Ford Jr.'s animated *Chair-A-Go-Go*, above right, is dramatically asymmetrical. Its seat cushion and the support underneath are horizontal and static, but everything else pushes and leans in one way or another. The backrest twists and slants to the right, a movement embellished by the rhythmic

sequence of rounded blue forms. In response, the oversized armrest on the left tugs the opposite way and slightly downward. The smaller right armrest pulls back to the right and a bit lower still. Finally, the foot on the left extends further than its counterpart on the right, leading the eye back to the left and bottom. Ford zigzags us through his space, playing one element against another, in a way that eventually results in a balanced resolution.

Generally, hair grows symmetrically, and hairstyles that retain the feeling result in a harmony between hair and head. Stylists who want to create a look with more interest defy that inherent symmetry to produce sculpted designs that are radically asymmetrical. Larry Hopkins's design, above left, is a stunning example. Similarly, the singular, graceful form of Olivier Rollins's lampshade design *Hommage à Coco Channel*, facing page, left, is unusually asymmetrical, featuring one long, large, even movement to the left, countered in weight by more compressed and intertwined movements on the right.

LARRY HOPKINS, *Asian Fusion,* 2002. Hair design. Model: Kyoko Masukyo. *Photo by Kelly Giezentanner. Courtesy of Ananda Hair Studio, Asheville, NC.*

RICHARD FORD, *Chair-A-Go-Go,* 1999. 32 x 40 x 34 inches (81.3 x 101.6 x 86.4 cm). Polychromed poplar, silk upholstery. *Photo by Bill Bachuber.*

■ EXERCISE 1

EXPLORING ASYMMETRY IN SIMPLE BLACK-AND-WHITE COLLAGE

This first exercise offers an easy way to begin experimenting with asymmetry. You'll compose using pure black and pure white only, use squares and rectangles only, and arrange elements in a long rectangular format. By eliminating the full range of visual forces, you focus the challenge. You'll produce several quick designs. Each will create a dialogue between elements on the left and elements on the right that results in a feeling of equilibrium.

What You Need

Ruler

Pencil

4 two-dimensional surfaces, such as paper, cardboard, mat board, canvas, or cloth

Collage materials that contain solid black (Magazines are ideally suited for this, but you may choose to use newspapers, cloth samples, or any relatively flat material that you can easily cut or tear and paste to a surface.)

Scissors

Adhesive (Acrylic medium [flat, gloss, or gel] works well. White craft glue is an inexpensive substitute.)

What You Do

1. With your pencil and ruler, mark off on each of your four surfaces a long horizontal rectangle, 2 inches (5.1 cm) tall by as long as your working surface allows (12 inches [30.5 cm] minimum; 18 inches [45.7 cm] would be ideal).

2. Scavenge through your sources for collage, and gather samples of absolute, stark black. Avoid very dark grays that aren't quite black, and avoid passages that are unevenly black or textured with non-black elements.

3. Cut the black elements into rectangles, squares, and thin bars that are all exactly 2 inches (5.1 cm) tall. Vary the width of the elements as much as you can. Make sure you have a couple that are relatively large. For example, if you're working on a surface that's 18 inches (45.7 cm) wide, cut some rectangles that are roughly 2 x 6 inches (5.1 x 15.2 cm).

4. Start a design in each of the marked-off rectangles by placing one of the larger black rectangles in each of the following positions: touching the left edge, a fraction of an inch (2.5 cm) inside the left edge, 1¹/₂ inches (3.8 cm) inside the right edge, and near the center of the space but clearly off center.

5. In each of the four design spaces, begin to place additional black rectangles, plus squares and bars, in response to the position of the initial large rectangle. Search for ways to achieve balance in the spaces, but avoid mirroring images from side to side. Instead, explore until you find other arrangements and relative placements that bring about balance.

■ EXERCISE 2

EXPLORING RADICAL ASYMMETRY IN MIXED MEDIA

Next, you'll develop an asymmetrical design using a wide range of visual forces (shape, color, texture, line, and mark), and media of your choice. The only rules are that you start with one powerful element on one side and that this element not be mirrored or even repeated again. Otherwise, you can arrange as you wish, as long as the resulting design is balanced and asymmetrical.

What You Need

Two-dimensional surface, such as paper, cardboard, mat board, canvas, or cloth; the size is up to you

Media and materials of your choice (You can work with any of the items used in earlier challenges in the book, such as paints, stamps and inks, or collage pieces, or you can choose another medium.)

What You Do

1. Establish one very large, powerful shape or cluster of shapes on one side of the surface. It should be large enough to dominate the space, engaging nearly one quarter of the surface area.

2. Experiment with introducing a variety of contrasting shapes elsewhere. Start by adding one additional shape, for example. Pause for a moment to experience the relationship between this new shape and its placement and the first shape, as well as the relationship between the two shapes and the edges of the design space.

3. Begin to ask yourself a series of questions about the arrangement. For example, does it feel lopsided? Do you sense that it's top heavy? Respond to your answers by adding more elements in places where you think they're needed or by altering existing elements and/or moving them around.

4. When the design is further along, ask additional questions. Does one area of the design feel overcrowded and claustrophobic? If so, remove or cover an element in that area, or respond by making other areas more crowded, too. Does another passage feel weak, tentative, or lacking in definition? If so, add an element or series of elements that

create strong contrasts, such as value, saturation, hard edges, or heavy texture.

5. Continue to arrange, respond, and rearrange. Juggle the design until the weight and force of the large and powerful original element is satisfyingly countered by the relationships of weights elsewhere in the space. Consider the design to be finished when the overall arrangement feels balanced and you're happy with the design.

CHAPTER 9

FOCAL EMPHASIS

Another traditional way of arranging a design is to organize elements in relation to a *focal point*. A focal point is the place of primary emphasis in a design, the place that exerts the most pressure. In addition to being the first place to which the eye is drawn, a focal point also serves as a place for the eye to return when it wants to pause or rest during its experience of a design. After pausing at "home base," it can set off on a second journey through the space, and a third, and so on.

You can establish a focal point and related points of emphasis in an infinite variety of ways. Any visual contrast can serve the purpose. All other forces and contrasts being equal, consider how the following kinds of relationships might do the trick:

• Contrast of scale (see figure 1). In a space scattered with small to medium-size ovals, for example, one relatively large oval might create quite a focal ruckus, pulling the eye right to it. The converse could work equally well. In a space full of medium to large ovals, one small one might speak the loudest.

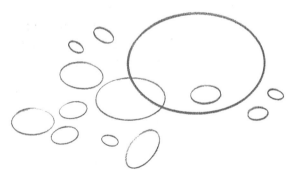

Figure 1

• Contrast of shape (see figure 2). Similarly, in a space full of ovals, one triangle would most certainly demand our attention.

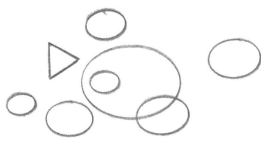

Figure 2

• Contrast of orientation (see figure 3). Imagine a space with a large cluster of identical little circles confined to one area, with ample white space all around. Take one of those little circles and place it outside the cluster—anyplace in the quiet area—and your eye will be drawn right to it.

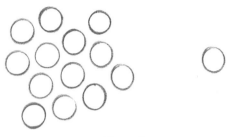

Figure 3

• Contrast of activity/passivity (see figure 4). Should most of the surface of a design be highly activated or textured, an area of stark, passive quiet will ironically become the focus of attention.

Figure 4

• Contrast of color (see figure 5). Any of the color contrasts covered in pages 68 through 93 can be used to establish focal emphasis. Consider contrast of saturation, for example. In a design full of varying degrees of neutralized color, a note of pure color will cry out for attention.

Figure 5

These are all examples of how to achieve focal emphasis by relying on the principle of unity and variety. In each example, the design is unified by one type of force or relationship, while the element that breaks the unity with the greatest variety stands out and commands attention.

Another way of establishing focal emphasis is by setting up a series of *directional thrusts* that point to the spot to be emphasized. These thrusts are often linear and are sometimes literally present and at other times implied. In other cases, shapes such as elongated triangles can be arrows that show us the way. Rhythmic repetitions of a motif can lead the eye on a movement or series of movements ending at the focal area as well.

In addition to featuring one focal area, most effective designs of this kind also establish a series of secondary points of emphasis. After all, what's the eye to do after it goes to and appreciates the focal area? Most designers set up secondary points of emphasis in a way that encourages the eye to visit the entire space in an intriguing and satisfying journey. These spots play a strong role in the design, but remain subordinate to the focal point. At times, these secondary points establish a clear hierarchy, so the viewer is led from one spot to the next. In this case, the designer is acting very much like a choreographer, establishing movement from point to point on a stage. At other times, the secondaries have no clear hierarchy, and the viewer is encouraged to find his or her own way through the design. In either case, these secondary areas, in combination with the focal point, activate the entire space.

Traditionally, designers in western European culture have placed focal points just off center (figure 6). The theory has been that this position is where the eye feels most comfortable, with dead center focal being too static (figure 7) and far-from-center focus being too weak (figure 8). Designers in the modernist era experimented with placing focal points and important secondary points on the very outside edge of their compositional space, and discovered those edges can be powerful places for focal emphasis as well (figure 9).

Arrangement according to focal emphasis is especially effective for certain design purposes, notably portraiture and designs that tell stories. For a portrait of a sitting subject, for example, painters tend to establish the head or even specific features as the focal area. In a composition that tells a story,

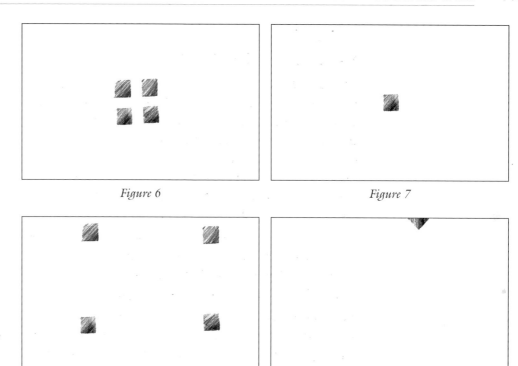

Figure 6

Figure 7

Figure 8

Figure 9

the designer usually leads us to the central figure or activity as the main focus. Or, think about advertising design, where the primary name or message is driven home to the viewer through a focal point or a series of focal emphases.

Examples

Organizing a design around a focal emphasis can be as simple as using one element or contrast to direct the viewer to a particular place in the space. Such is the case with Don Davis's wheel-thrown ceramic *Pitcher*, below. This pared-down, elegant form is unified by a surface that's overwhelmingly clean, smooth, and glossy. The exception is one passage where an organic texture stands in sharp contrast to the rest of the form's surface. This relatively small area of variety commands attention and becomes the focus.

In Lynn Whipple's collage and assemblage *Mabel*, right, color creates the focal point. The figure's red hat is the largest of two red shapes in the design, the only two

LYNN WHIPPLE, *Mabel,* 1999. 12 x 12 x 2 inches (30.5 x 30.5 x 5 cm). Collage, acrylic, pencil, found objects, altered found images on wood. *Photo by Randall Smith.*

DON DAVIS, *Pitcher,* 1998. 10 x 6 x 5 inches (25.4 x 15.3 x 12.7 cm). Wheel thrown porcelain with pulled handle; interior glazed, exterior metallic oxide spray with separating glaze. *Photo by Evan Bracken.*

elements of saturated color in the composition. The red hat joins with the neckline, head, and hair of the figure below to form the primary passage in Whipple's narrative. From here, she directs viewers around the arrangement, starting with the second red note, moving to the large wire loop, and continuing to the sliver of black on the right and back up to the focal point.

A series of directional thrusts or *converging lines* establishes a primary focal emphasis in Sandra D. Lloyd's oil painting *Boat and Rocks, Stonington, #11*, facing page. The focal point here is literally that: a point in space, rather than an identifiable shape, form, or mark.

SANDRA D. LLOYD, *Boats and Rocks, Stonington, #11,* 2001. 7 x 5½ inches (17.8 x 14 cm). Oil on gessoed paper. *Photo by Beach Photo and Video.*

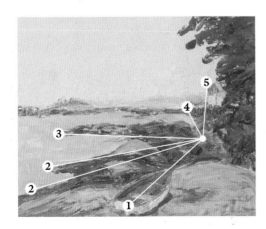

(1) *The angle of the boat allows it to act as a directional arrow that points to the focal area.*

(2) *The top edges of the first two land bars join the boat in pointing up and to the right.*

(3) *The bottom edge of the third bar points to the right and slightly down.*

(4) *The shape of the water dips down at the last minute, pointing to the focal point.*

(5) *Even the building in the distance tilts slightly to the right, so its left edge points downward to the spot of convergence.*

REMBRANDT VAN RIJN, *The Militia Company of Frans Banning Cocq,* 1642.
12 feet 2 inches x 14 feet 7 inches (3.7 x 4.5 m). Oil on canvas. *Rijksmuseum, Amsterdam, Holland.*

JIMMY CHEN, 2003.
Sushi arrangement.
Photo by keithwright.com.
Courtesy of Wasabi Japanese
Cuisine, Asheville, NC.

In *The Militia Company of Frans Banning Cocq*, also called *The Night Watch*, by Rembrandt van Rijn, facing page, the eye goes right to a cluster of activity near the middle of the space. The head of the main figure dressed in black is the primary focus. Rembrandt uses a variety of visual forces to direct attention to this area. In a design dominated by highly neutralized color, the largest and most crisply defined area of saturated color—red—occurs in the central figure's cape. The most extreme contrast of value takes place where the central figure's white collar butts up against his black garment. A little gray line connects this figure's right shoulder to the white hat and head of the secondary figure to his right.

Then, the direction of the secondary figure's gaze points the eye right back to the central figure. Rembrandt's expert arrangement takes off from here, using a variety of secondary points to lead the eye on a satisfying journey.

You'll find similar dynamics at work in a chef's arrangement of sushi on a plate, above, where the shrimp and green garnish serve as focal point, not only because of their scale, but because the angles in the rest of the arrangement point directly to them.

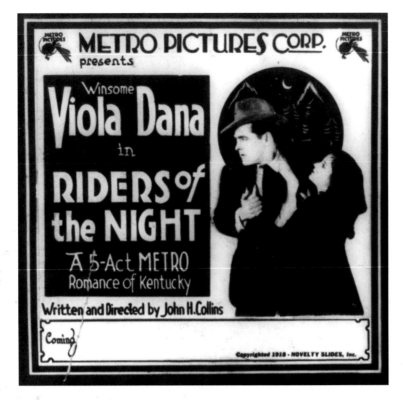

The *Riders of the Night* motion picture poster design, top left, is built around a focal emphasis—the hero—that's just off center. We're drawn right to his head by a curving, backwards "C" movement formed by the heroine's arms and his neck. The heroine's gaze directs us to the focal point as well, and the hero even points his own finger toward himself to show us the way. The angled movement of the italicized "f" in the text gives us a final nudge toward the focal point in this deceptively powerful and complex design.

Art Garst's *Retaining-Wall Bench*, bottom left, is unified by a repetition of stone forms that are similar in scale and shape and placed in a repeating horizontal orientation. The one significant element that doesn't fit this system is the stone that forms the backrest of the bench. It's both larger than the rest and it's set up on its side, so we can see its breadth of surface. These differences make the backrest not only functional, but also the visual centerpiece of the entire arrangement.

A design with a focal emphasis established by contrast of value is John L. Skau's rug design *Fido*, facing page. What's the focal area in this space? The white quarter moon to the right and above center. The elements that force the eye toward it include the dog's mouth, lined with hard-edged, triangular teeth that frame the moon. In addition, several in a series of blue bars on the right point right to it.

Riders of the Night, 1918. Motion picture advertisement.
Courtesy of the Library of Congress.

ART GARST, *Retaining-Wall Bench,* 1998. Approximately 10 x 25 feet (3 x 7.5 m). Dry stone paving, sandstone set on crushed stone and quarry screenings. *Photo by David Reed.*

JOHN L. SKAU, *Fido,* 1986. 59 x 71 x 1 inches
(149.9 x 180.3 x 2.5 cm). Cotton fabrics, twine,
canvas foundation, fake fur, sewing thread. *Photo by
John L. Skau.*

Exercises

As discussed with other exercises, you can create a design by sticking to a plan, beginning with a loose idea and improvising, or beginning with no plan at all and responding to a series of events. The following exercises explore this range. The first and its two variations are somewhat structured; the second is more open ended.

■ EXERCISE 1

FOCAL EMPHASIS JUST OFF CENTER

Here's your chance to experience designing with a focal point in the traditional off-center placement. Do the exercise twice, using a different visual element as the central focus each time.

What You Need

Collage materials you can easily cut or tear and paste
    to a surface, such as construction paper, magazines,
    newspapers, and cloth samples

Access to a photocopier (optional)

Scissors (optional)

Adhesive (Acrylic medium [flat, gloss, or gel] works well.
    White craft glue is an inexpensive substitute.)

2 rectangular surfaces, such as flat pieces of paper,
    cardboard, or mat board, each the same size and shape

Rubber stamps (optional)

Rubber stamp pads (one or more colors) (optional)

What You Do

1. Cut, rip, or otherwise generate a series of simple shapes that vary in scale and character. For example, you might cut small, medium, and large versions of a square, triangle, and oval, along with a number of organic shapes. You can vary these in color, texture, and edge as well.

2. Reproduce the shapes by photocopying them or tracing and cutting them again, so you can use them in several variations.

3. Place one of these shapes on a surface as your focal point, using one of the four traditional off-center placements.

4. Begin to add other shapes that have varying weight and character. You can do this at random, according to an idea you have in mind, or in response to the "feel" of the focal element.

5. Step back, get a sense of the arrangement, and respond again by introducing new elements, replacing existing ones, and perhaps eliminating others. You also have the option, at this point, to embellish the design with stamped elements for variety.

6. Continue until the space feels both intriguing and resolved. This resolution should include a dominant focal point and a series of other strong points that encourage the eye to move through and experience the entire space.

7. Using the elements you photocopied or traced and recut and a surface that's identical in shape and size, create another design. Work again with the traditional focal placement, this time using a radically different element as the point of emphasis. For example, if you used a small square of highly saturated color as the focal point in your first design, try using a large but very dull element this time.

Variation: Focal Emphasis on Outside Edge

This time, try working with a focal point (and perhaps other major points of interest) on the outside edge of the surface. Remember that any element that engages the outside edge increases in power and prominence, which make this a fascinating design idea to explore. Use the same materials as in Exercise 1 (including the same photocopied or traced elements, if possible), and engage in the same process. The only exception is that you'll begin by placing your focal-point shape on an outside edge.

Variation: Focal Emphasis in Weak Placement

Here's another variation that presents an unorthodox challenge: arrange a design with a focal emphasis in what is considered to be a weak placement—a compositional no-man's land. As you've gathered from earlier exercises, weak placement does not mean just off center, on the outside edge, or dead center (often a very strong placement in symmetrical arrangements). Instead, weak placement means away from center, but not all the way to an edge. The strongest of the weak possibilities would be to place the focus element in the no-man's land near the top, especially the top left (remember, all else being equal, our eye likes to start there). So, to increase the challenge, use one of the other three placements instead. Use the same materials as in Exercise 1 (including the same photocopied or traced elements, if possible), and engage in the same process.

■ EXERCISE 2

FINDING RATHER THAN PLANNING A FOCAL EMPHASIS

Instead of planning or imposing a focal point at the outset, this exercise encourages you to "discover" a focal point—and the arrangement around it—as you go. Let out-of-control events play a large role in the process. Welcome them. You'll act as responder and editor. Keep in mind that if something "accidental" occurs (an unplanned drop of paint, a misplaced collage piece) and you choose to keep it in the design rather than change or remove it, then it's not really an accident anymore. In the end, the composition can have the same organizational strengths that a "planned" design does.

What You Need

You can create this design on any surface, out of any materials, and on any scale and in any format you wish. The instructions are tailored to working on the flat, rectangular surfaces we've been using, but feel free to adapt them.

Collage materials you can easily cut or tear, paste to a surface, and photocopy, such as construction paper, magazines, newspapers, and cloth samples (Start with collage materials, then add other media, if you like.)

Scissors (optional)

Adhesive (Acrylic medium [flat, gloss, or gel] works well. White craft glue is an inexpensive substitute.)

What You Do

1. Cut or tear a series of at least eight shapes out of the collage material.

2. Using the shapes as a starting point, begin to generate activity on your design surface in a manner that you don't control. For example, put your surface on the floor and drop the shapes onto it from several feet above, allowing them to find their own placement. Toss the shapes over your shoulder onto the surface. Close your eyes and shuffle them around on the surface. Or, ask someone else to place them on the surface.

3. As you've done before, step back and spend a minute taking in the random configuration. Does one area intrigue you most? It might be a candidate for focal-point status. Close your eyes and shuffle the elements around some more, and ask the same question. Continue until you decide that one element will be your focus.

4. Now, engage in the design process in response to the focal point. Add more elements, alter others, and perhaps eliminate others altogether. Remember, what you're hoping for is an arrangement that encourages the eye to move around the space, taking it all in in a satisfying way.

5. If you reach a point where you're not yet satisfied with the design but don't know what to do next, try initiating a few more random events to shake things up and open new possibilities.

6. As you move through the design process, if you find that a new area is more intriguing as a central focus than the original one, consider abandoning your first focal point in favor of a new one.

7. Continue the process until you feel you have a design that's satisfyingly organized around a focal emphasis.

RAPHAEL, *The Canigiani Holy Family,*
c. 1505-1506. 51 ½ x 42 ⅛ inches
(131 x 107 cm). Oil on panel.
Alte Pinakothek, Munich, Germany.

CHAPTER 10

UNDERLYING SHAPES

Whether you're setting out to create a design and need a place to start or you're looking for a way to pull together a design that's feeling disjointed, here's an approach you can use. Distill your design into an arrangement of a few simple shapes, then use them to hold your design together. Those underlying shapes work something like a jigsaw puzzle to engage your entire design space and make it feel complete.

Examples

One of the classic examples of a composition arranged according to an underlying shape is *The Canigiani Holy Family*, facing page, by the Italian renaissance painter Raphael. Its underlying structure is as clear and powerful as can be. All the important elements, both visually and narratively, are clustered inside one large, central triangle. The base of the triangle rests near the bottom of the space, and the lines of the triangle extend to the top, near center. Notice, too, that the spaces to the left and right of the triangle are

CHEF ALFRED PORTALE, 2002. Architectural food arrangement. *Photo by Anna Williams for* Food & Wine, *September 2002.*

JEAN BANAS, *Thrust,* 1998. 30 x 24 inches (76.2 x 61 cm). Mixed water media on paper. *Photo by Beach Photo and Video.*

both triangular in nature. The entire design space is engaged by these three interlocking triangles that provide a feeling of completion.

Anna Williams's photo of an architectural food arrangement, left, mimics Raphael's design to a T, only this time in three dimensions. All the elements are clustered into a pyramid shape that gives strong unity and bold clarity to the culinary composition.

Contemporary painter Jean Banas structures elements similarly in her mixed-media design *Thrust*, above. She starts with a three-triangle structure as well. This time, the central and largest triangle is inverted and cropped, so its implied apex lies below the bottom of the space. Its base is located roughly at the top of the space, though the edges of the triangle become lost and found in places, offering an intriguing sense of ambiguity. There are triangles on each side as well, which join with the first to fill the entire design space.

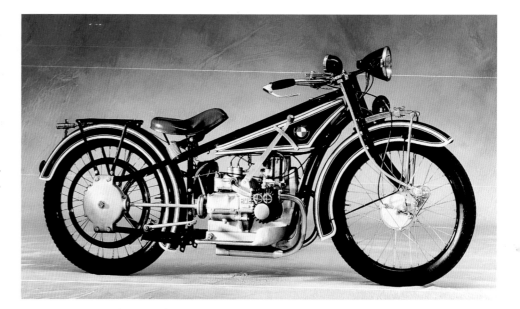

BMW, *R 32 Motorcycle,* 1926.
BMW Corporate Communications Archive.

BMW, *R 50/5 Motorcycle,* c. 1969-73.
BMW Corporate Communications Archive.

Compare two classic BMW motorcycles to see just how powerful the principle of underlying shape can be in design—and to see how it can be used to create different moods. Both motorcycles are structured around one large foundation shape. The *R 32*, top, is built around a triangle that holds disparate elements together visually. The top side of the triangle runs on a diagonal from near the center of the rear tire to the handlebar near the front, creating the feeling that this motorcycle is revved and ready to take off. In the *R 50/5*, bottom, the main body joins with the exhaust pipe and the rear of the seat to create a parallelogram that reads as roughly rectangular. The result is a machine that feels powerfully strong and stable.

In John Twachtman's composition *Gloucester Harbor*, facing page, underneath the soft, atmospheric representation of a New England harbor are three big, bold triangles.

JOHN TWACHTMAN,
Gloucester Harbor, c. 1901.
25 X 25 inches (63.5 x 63.5
cm). Oil on canvas. *Courtesy of
the Canajoharie Library and Art
Gallery, Canajoharie, NY.*

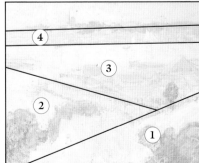

(1) *The first starts at the center of the design's right edge.*

(2) *Triangle number two uses a portion of the top of the first
triangle to form its base.*

(3) *The third triangle sits above triangle number two.*

(4) *Two horizontal bars complete the space above, making this an
underlying structure of five big, simple shapes.*

Hannelore Baron, *Untitled,* 1978. Fiber collage. *Courtesy of the Estate of Hannelore Baron.*

Hannelore Baron's mixed-media collage *Untitled*, 1978, facing page, shows yet another possibility for organizing with underlying shapes: using a series of horizontal bars that form a grid. This grid engages the entire space and serves as the structure in which a variety of elements relate.

Exercises

■ EXERCISE 1

STAMPING TO EXPLORE UNDERLYING SHAPE

What You Need

A flat, rectangular surface, such as a piece of paper, cardboard, or mat board in a size of your choice

Pencil

Several rubber stamps

Several rubber stamp pads

What You Do

1. Review the examples showcased in this chapter, and pick one of the underlying shapes used by one of the designers, or come up with one of your own.

2. Draw the shape on the surface. This large shape will create one, two, or three other shapes out of the remaining space on the surface (see figure 1 for an example; this series of underlying shapes comes from the John Twachtman painting on page 153). Outline the additional shapes with the pencil as well. This will help you consider their potential role as part of the design, too.

3. Generate some activity in the space by stamping in any way you wish. You might choose to make this a purely formal arrangement, or you might want to arrange elements so they tell a story, reveal an internal state, or send a message of some kind. Use as broad a range of stamp shapes and ink colors as you like.

4. Cluster a dominant amount of activity in one dominant underlying shape (see figure 2).

5. Stamp in the areas outside the dominant underlying shape as well, making sure to keep these stamped elements subordinate to those in the dominant shape (see figure 3).

6. Continue adding, layering, and covering until you're satisfied with the design and it holds together powerfully according to its underlying shapes.

Figure 2

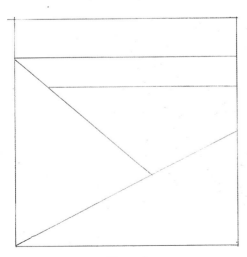

Figure 1

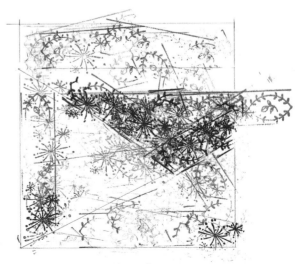

Figure 3

■ EXERCISE 2

CONTRAST OF TEXTURE AND VALUE WITH AN UNDERLYING GRID

Whether you're working in two or three dimensions, designing according to an underlying grid is a very simple, powerful, and eloquent way of organizing a space. A grid offers a regular pattern of shapes that supports the addition of new elements. It naturally compartmentalizes space by designating sections that relate to one another. The uniformity of a grid also contributes to a feeling of unity. In this exercise, you'll work within the confines of a grid while exploring the contrasts of texture and value.

What You Need

Pencil

Ruler

A two-dimensional surface, such as paper, cardboard, mat board, canvas, or cloth

Collage materials featuring a variety of textures (magazines, newspapers, cloth samples, or any relatively flat material you can easily cut or tear and paste to a surface)

Scissors (optional)

Access to a black-and-white photocopier or a scanner and a black-and-white printer

Adhesive (Acrylic medium [flat, gloss, or gel] works well. White craft glue is an inexpensive substitute. You can also assemble this collage using an alternative technique, such as sewing your pieces together.)

What You Do

1. With the pencil and ruler (or freehand, if you prefer), draw a grid on your surface.

2. Gather a series of collage elements that contain a wide and interesting variety of textures.

3. Run your collage elements through a black-and-white photocopier. This will eliminate all color contrast except value, so you can isolate texture as your design element and the underlying grid as your design structure.

4. Begin placing collage elements in various compartments of the grid. As the elements activate the design space with their different textures, start to contrast "busy" passages with "quiet" ones.

5. Notice how the textures in some compartments contrast with the textures in others, and how the contrasting compartments begin to relate to one another. Think of them as being engaged in a dialogue. Notice, too, how the grid underneath holds the space together.

6. Continue to add, subtract, and rearrange collage elements until you feel a resolution. Your finished design should feature an intriguing pattern of busy and quiet unified by the grid framework underneath.

CHAPTER 11

CRITIQUE

We began this book with a definition of design: the arrangement of visual elements in space. By now, you've been introduced to all aspects of that definition and have a good idea of the different purposes a design can serve. You know the various forms the design process can take. You're very familiar with the raw materials you work with when designing, you understand the nature and dynamics of a design space, and you've viewed examples of and worked hands-on with basic principles of arrangement that can help you organize designs effectively.

In this final chapter, we'll summarize it all as we analyze and appreciate a number of wonderful designs that show-case various media and design purposes. Until now, we've talked about designs in relation to a single idea or principle covered in a particular chapter or section. Now, we'll respond to some designs more holistically and consider each on a variety of levels.

You can approach this discussion in one of two ways. If you like, read the text for each example and refer to the image each step of the way to understand it. Or, you might try another approach. As you move from example to example, look at the image before reading the accompanying text, and analyze the design for yourself. Take your time. Again, think about what the design purpose might be, what process you think the artist undertook, what the visual elements are and how they're used, how the elements relate to the space, and what organizing principles are at work. Write your responses down if you like. Then, when you're finished, read the accompanying text. It's likely your analysis will have much in common with mine. Perhaps you'll notice points I've missed. And, likely, you'll have contributions to make that are uniquely yours. In any event, you should find this process of analysis and critique illuminating. Enjoy!

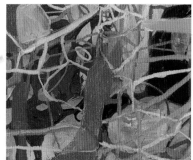
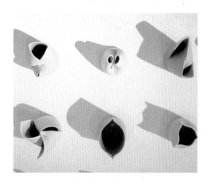

Detail of bottom left corner of the Rembrandt, facing page, inverted.

Franz Kline, *Figure 8,*
1952. 80⅞ x 63⅜ inches
(205.4 x 161 cm).
Oil on canvas.
Collection of Harry W. and
Mary Margaret Anderson.

COMPARISON

Figure 8, Franz Kline
A Woman Asleep, Rembrandt van Rijn

A great way to learn about the concepts we've discussed throughout this book is to compare designs from different cultures and time periods or designs that serve radically different purposes, analyzing their similarities as well as their differences. In the introduction, we paired Mozell Benson's African-American quilt and Piet Mondrian's abstract painting in this way (see pages 10 and 11). Now, let's look at another pair of "kindred spirits."

These two compositions look and feel remarkably similar. Above left is *Figure 8,* a nonrepresentational painting executed by American Franz Kline in 1951. The other composition, above right, could easily be another one of Kline's black-and-white paintings, but it's actually something quite different: a cropped and turned-on-its-side detail from the bottom corner of Rembrandt's ink drawing, *A Woman Asleep,* executed in Holland in 1654. It's shown in its entirety on the facing page.

The significant difference between these two designs is that of purpose. Kline's purpose is formal—to show how lines and shapes can tell a story all by themselves. For him, the arrangement of visual elements is the subject of his design. He's not depicting anything in the natural world; he's creating an independent reality. In Rembrandt's day, however, designs always had a descriptive or narrative purpose. In *A Woman Asleep*, his primary use of line is to describe a woman at rest. But beyond this difference in purpose, the designs have much in common, beginning with the fact that both Rembrandt and Kline use line to create shapes and establish rhythms in intriguing and satisfying ways. And both delight in exploring what line alone can express.

In *Figure 8*, line creates shape, indicates direction and movement, and establishes emphasis through changes in weight and edge. The composition is organized and unified through repetition of an oval motif, with the diversity of the ovals adding compelling variety. In addition to working with line, Kline also experiments with positive and negative relationships. While he primarily uses black as a positive element, occasionally he paints white over the black, creating a curious ambiguity between positive and negative. Also, Kline's finished piece clearly reflects his process of acting and responding as he worked. You can see, for example, where he veiled or nearly obliterated black elements as he created the painting. Finally, the large, double oval that forms the figure eight works as an organizing force for the design.

A Woman Asleep might seem as nonrepresentational as *Figure 8* if not for the series of marks clustered together at the top left that symbolize the girl's head and face. Notice how this cluster of activity serves as the focal point because it creates something recognizable and because of its placement in the upper-left portion of the design space. Notice, too, how the larger, bolder cluster underneath attracts the eye through the intensity of its mark and line. The lower cluster also serves as a foundation for the head's visual weight. Next, a rhythmic sequence of light contour lines beginning at the head indicate successive layers of fabric as it moves to the bottom right of the space. Finally, notice how Rembrandt clusters all the design elements into one large, organizing triangle: from the head down to the foot, left from the foot through a series of points that form a long horizontal, and finally up from the left end of that horizontal to the head again.

REMBRANDT VAN RIJN, *A Woman Asleep,* c. 1654. Approx. 9 3/4 x 8 inches (24.5 x 20.3 cm). Brush and wash. *British Museum, London, Great Britain. Copyright Art Resource/Art Resource, NY.*

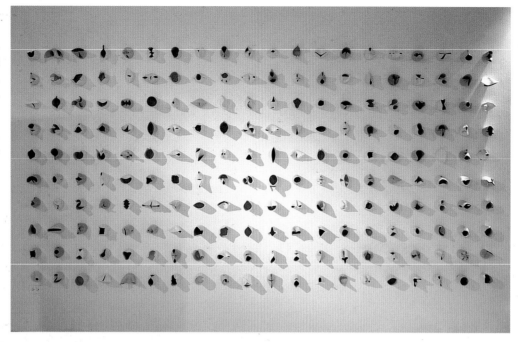

ERIN JONES, *Recurrence,*
2003. Approx. 7 x 13 feet
(2.1 x 4 m).
Porcelain with terra sigillata.
Photo by Dan Harris.

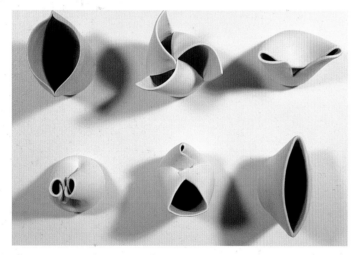

ANALYSIS

Recurrence, **Erin Jones**

Erin Jones's ceramic installation is a striking example of design as a dialogue among a community of visual elements in a shared space. *Recurrence* consists of 200 small ceramic forms (4 x 3 1/2 x 3 1/2 inches [10.2 x 8.9 x 8.9 cm]) installed in a rectangular configuration on a gallery wall. Each began with the same wheel-thrown cylinder. This repetition of form, plus the fact that the forms are installed in horizontal and vertical rows of equal spacing, effectively unifies the design. Jones creates variety and tension by manipulating the tops of the forms, creating a wide range of permutations. She pinched some, pressed others, and cut the majority down the sides, so she could twist, fold, and rejoin those portions into a rich variety of new forms. This diversity creates an interesting series of relationships, enhanced by the rhythmic pattern of dark shapes inside the forms. The shadows the pieces cast on the wall create new shapes that echo the forms, lending additional vibration to the individual notes. The result is a visual symphony organized according to repetition of motif.

In addition to its primary purpose of experimenting with form, Jones's design has an emotive purpose. Her interesting choices regarding color support it. Notice that the palette in her design is limited to pastel variations of the three primary colors. They're very pleasing, gentle colors, often associated with femininity, making them ironically at odds with the very masculine, monumental feel of the large installation format. Consider how the impact of the design would be different if it had been executed in black and white, or how the dialogue among the elements would be affected if Jones had used a full range of pure, saturated color instead.

ANALYSIS

Jungle Fusion II, Mary Bero

If you think of embroidery as an old-fashioned craft used simply to decorate and adorn, take a look at Mary Bero's *Jungle Fusion II*, and think again. Her embroidered cotton, silk, and rayon panel is meant to be decorative, but her purposes extend beyond that, to the narrative and emotive. To achieve them, Bero employs a wide array of organizing principles that act in concert, resulting in a fiber composition of great complexity and sophistication.

In pure design terms, *Jungle Fusion II* exhibits a very loose feeling of symmetry. Its central axis starts with a single figure at the top, then slices between the palm tree trunk and the head of the blue-haired woman in the middle. The axis follows her arm down through an eye/leg combination on the left and an arm/flower pair on the right. But the tweaking of this symmetry is substantial, creating a great deal of tension in the space. To counter that tension, Bero employs other organizing principles. A loose, grid-like pattern of rectangles acts as a large underlying shape structure, locking elements together in jigsaw-puzzle fashion. Ovals and modified ovals recur throughout as a unifying motif. The recurrence of consistent marks made by the embroidery stitches helps unify, as well. The design also features a woven pattern of warm/cold contrast; notice how areas of warm reds, oranges, yellows, and warm greens alternate with areas dominated by cool reds, purples, and blues.

All of this organization enables Bero's design to function powerfully on various levels. Emotively, the arrangement is very lively and bold, even frenetic in its energy. Great variety in texture and pattern and in her use of colors from throughout the wheel contribute to the feeling. Narratively, *Jungle Fusion II* juxtaposes a variety of recognizable, figurative forms and challenges the viewer to interpret and respond. Figures in the main panel seem to be related to the more abstract, primitive, black-and-white counterparts in the border areas. Some figurative forms read as volumes in space, while others flatten into mask-like states. Others merge texturally with their patterned surroundings. Disembodied parts float in surreal fashion. While open to a variety of responses and interpretations, *Jungle Fusion II* presents a challenging and somewhat unsettling vision of the interconnectedness and likely merger of disparate cultures, both East and West, past and present.

MARY BERO, *Jungle Fusion II,* 1990.
9 ½ x 7 ½ inches (24.1 x 19.1 cm). Cotton, silk, rayon; embroidered.
The Minneapolis Institute of Arts, Minneapolis, MN. Gift of the Textile Council.

KARL FRITSCH, *Ring,* 1993-1995. Approx. 2 ¼ inches (6 cm) tall. Silver, copper, cold enamel, glass stones, crystal. *Photo by the artist.*

ANALYSIS

Ring, Karl Fritsch

Karl Fritsch's *Ring* is a wonderful example of contemporary mixed-media sculpture. While his design had to meet minimal utilitarian requirements (the piece needs to fit and stay on a finger), its primary purpose is to be decorative, whether it's adorning a finger or attracting viewers in a gallery.

The design is roughly symmetrical, though the balance is delicate and precarious. Four blue gems sit atop towers made of metal and glass, two on each side. They're supported by a large, flat shelf covered with blue stones that echo the gems above. The open, cylindrical ring form provides the central axis.

The ring's design is also based on repetition of a shape motif: a modified oval with multifaceted edges. You see it in the gemstones, the glass chips, the blue stones, and in one other delightful and unexpected place. Fritsch has hammered the ring cylinder so its edges are no longer round but multifaceted, creating the final, super-sized instance of the motif. This modification in the shape of the ring serves another important purpose. The modified oval feels as if it's less likely to roll than a perfect circle would, making it more plausible visually for the ring to support and balance the architectural adornments above.

ANALYSIS

Room Divider, Jill Henrietta Davis

Jill Henrietta Davis creates contemporary glass sculpture in the guise of a screen in *Room Divider.* As is the case with Fritsch's ring, facing page, Davis's design serves a utilitarian purpose—in this instance, to section off one area of space from another. But if functionality had been Davis's primary design purpose, she certainly could have accomplished it without going through the difficulties of blowing, cutting, polishing, and assembling the fragile material of glass. Instead, her purpose is largely decorative. To achieve it, she establishes a number of very subtle and somewhat unorthodox relationships meant to challenge and intrigue.

At first glance, the design might seem to consist simply of a balanced, grid-like pattern of rectangles alternating horizontally and vertically. Its bilateral symmetry holds from left to right, but deviates from top to bottom. The top edge lines up predictably to form a horizontal, while the bottom edge diverges, forming a zigzag pattern instead. Because of this, our experience of the space is fixed and static at the top, but relatively open and airy at the bottom. In addition, the screen's directional movement is absolutely vertical at the top, but gently sloping at the bottom. While the transparency of the glass and the spaces throughout the divider feel open and fluid, the bottom slope causes the design to feel very different when experienced from the front side than when experienced from the back. From the front, the screen curves very gently away as it rises, creating a feeling of expansion, comfort, and air. From the back it curves up and toward the viewer, pressing in and dividing the space more powerfully.

JILL HENRIETTA DAVIS, *Room Divider,* 1998. 72 x 48 x 6 inches (182.9 x 121.9 x 15.3 cm). Blown, cut, polished and assembled glass. *Photo by artist.*

WILLIAM D. SARNI,
Wood Duck, 1990.
7 x 13 x 6 inches
(17.8 x 33 x 15.2 cm).
Native white pine, acrylic paint.
Photo by artist.

Commas repeat in a sequence.

Partial circles zigzag from left to right.

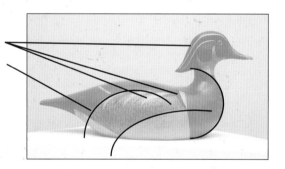

The negative areas established by the decoy's forms are elegant and rounded as well.

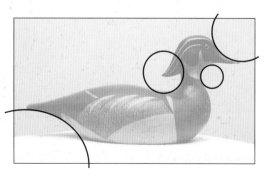

ANALYSIS

Wood Duck, William D. Sarni

If you've never looked at a wildfowl decoy as a piece of decorative as well as utilitarian sculpture, consider William D. Sarni's *Wood Duck*, and you're in for a treat.

In both its three-dimensional form and its two-dimensional surface decoration, *Wood Duck* is a design that's unified by an array of gently rounded elements. In three dimensions, notice the very elegant, positive forms of the large oval body, the horn-of-plenty shape and movement of the neck, and the circular underpinning of the head.

Sarni's surface decoration consists of rhythmic repetition of both comma-shaped and partial-circle motifs.

Finally, notice that Sarni's color choices are limited to very neutral earth tones, which not only unify the design, but suit the utilitarian requirement that it blend with colors in nature.

ANALYSIS

Keeping You Close to My Heart,
Olga Dvigoubsky Cinnamon

Olga Dvigoubsky Cinnamon's beaded doll is primarily a decorative object, and it's a piece of "eye candy" at that. But it has some secondary purposes, too. It's descriptive (its form is recognizably human) and emotive (its shape and surface patterns feel playful and tender). And it has a hidden utilitarian purpose as well: the top half of the body opens up to serve as a container for special mementos (thus the design's title).

This lively composition is unified by several organizing principles. It features bilateral symmetry that holds the arrangement together, while elements that don't quite fit the symmetrical system make the design surprising and exciting. Color contrasts of temperature and value work in unison. Dark, highly saturated purples, blues, and greens serve as foil for lighter purples and greens that vibrate nicely, and for intermittent, intense warm notes of red, orange, and golden yellow that pop out on the legs, skirt, and headdress.

Look further, and you'll also notice numerous little rhythmic sequences that repeat circular and rectangular motifs. You'll notice large, underlying shapes, too. The triangular skirt, cropped at the top; the inverted triangle of the torso, cropped at the bottom; and, most fundamentally, a large heart shape implied by the two arms. This last shape neatly and succinctly reinforces the design's narrative theme, *Keeping You Close to My Heart.*

OLGA DVIGOUBSKY CINNAMON,
Keeping You Close to My Heart,
2000. 10 x 4 x 1½ inches
(25.4 x 10.2 x 3.8 cm).
Waxed linen thread, glass beads, cotton fabric stuffing; crocheted. *Photo by Jeff Owen.*

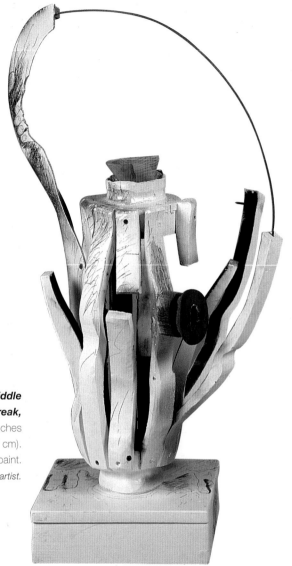

TIM MURRAY, *Middle Eastern Coffee Break,* 2002. 34 x 23 x 18 inches (86.4 x 58.4 x 45.7 cm). Wood, pencil, paint. *Collection of artist.*

We'll conclude our conversation by looking at two more pairs of kindred spirits. This first one demonstrates the similarities between working in two and three dimensions.

COMPARISON

Untitled (White Roma), Cy Twombly
Middle Eastern Coffee Break, Tim Murray

Both of these designs could very well have been titled, *Line and Mark as Subject*. Each is clearly formal, or decorative, in purpose. Both artists explore the expressive power of line and mark when they're arranged in a design space. And both limit color to emphasize contrasts of line, mark, and shape.

Twombly's painting consists of a frenzied series of impressions scratched with the tip of a pencil into a surface covered with white house paint. These marks are often veiled or obliterated by additional applications of paint, and more marks are added. Twombly continuously acted and responded in this way until he sensed a satisfying resolution to the design. Some marks may have had specific meaning for the artist. Notice, for example, the numerals "58" and the word "Roma" at the bottom left, or other instances where lines intersect or loop to form elements that look like letters: "H," "O," "A," "E," "P," or "M." But as much as these elements may hint at a planned narrative, Twombly's process was much more stream of consciousness; the story he's telling is largely subconscious and internal.

Murray's wood sculpture is similar in purpose, subject, and process, but the design is executed in three dimensions. It also works on two levels simultaneously.

First, the forms that make up *Middle Eastern Coffee Break* are all linear. Long strips of wood rise up from the cylindrical base to indicate movement and direction. Some wiggle gently and reattach themselves to another cylindrical form at the top. Others never make the journey intact; they're instead cut in two and left in fragmentary states. Still others meander to the outside of the center to indicate movements up and to the left and right. The most prominent of these strips—the one that represents a spout, on the left—curves back toward the center just a bit at the top. Here, it spawns a very thin, elegantly curved linear element that loops right and then down to latch onto a short strip on the right. With this, Murray showcases the ability of line to make shape; the large negative loop is one of the highlights of the design.

CY TWOMBLY, *Untitled*
(White Roma), 1958.
52 x 62 inches
(132.1 x 157.5 cm).
Oil, crayon, pencil on canvas.
Collection of David Geffen,
Los Angeles, CA.

Second, Murray likes to think of his forms as two-dimensional surfaces to draw on. Notice the expressive range of line and mark that adorn different areas of the arrangement. He leaves black marks on white painted surfaces, just as Twombly does in his painting. Also, bits of recognizable forms (note the fingertips that appear on the spout shape) hint at a narrative, but they remain subordinate. The result is another composition that reveals stream-of-consciousness processing in which the artist delights in what line and mark can do.

There are also differences in how these two designs are organized. Twombly's composition is unified by the similarity of the width and slant of the marks throughout. It's also organized by a series of rhythmic sequences that run on diagonals, from lower left to upper right. In contrast, Murray's arrangement is held together by the rhythmic sequence of the dancing wooden planks at the bottom and by its asymmetrical arrangement. Notice how the design is weighted to the right by the cluster of wood strips that protrude in the middle. This push is countered at the top by the one long plank and the leftward tilt of the negative loop shape and at the bottom by one little plank that tilts left, as well.

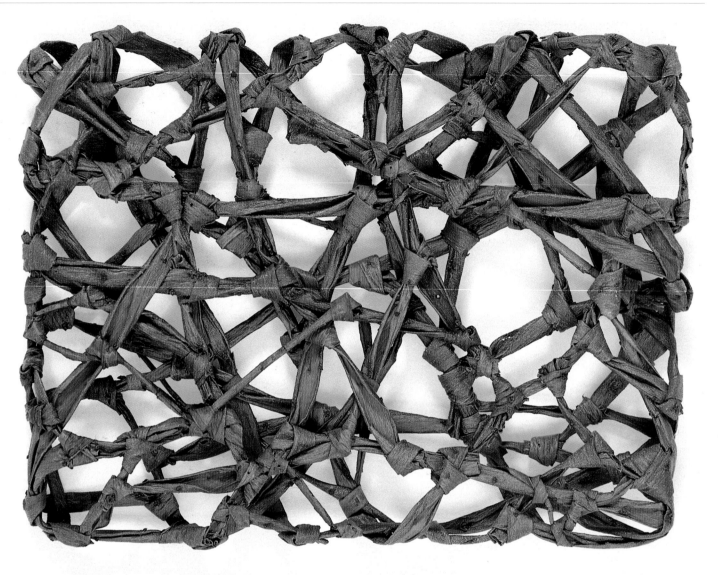

HISAKO SEKIJIMA,
Bound Space, 1997.
18½ x 14 x 3 inches
(47 x 35.6 x 7.6 cm).
Knotted and plaited fiber.
Photo by Tom Grotta.

Our final pairing demonstrates that exciting design is exciting design—no matter what tradition you work in or what materials you work with.

COMPARISON

Bound Space, Hisako Sekijima
Field of View, Terry Winters

Terry Winters is a contemporary American artist who works in the tradition of Western fine-art painting. His *Field of View* is executed in the materials of that tradition: oil paint applied to stretched linen canvas. Hisako Sekijima is a contemporary Japanese basket weaver and fiber artist who works with materials associated with the fine crafts. Her purely decorative, nonfunctional *Bound Space* is made from woven and knotted apricot fiber.

In spite of the wide gap separating the two artists' traditions and materials, the two designs are strikingly similar. Both consist of a series of looping movements that repeat and weave in and out and over and under one another. These movements seem to create modified oval shapes on the surface, but other woven patterns underneath break the loops into smaller and smaller shapes. The result in each case is an intricately woven space that feels alive with movement and depth. Both alternate between stopping the viewer at the surface and letting the viewer in. In both spaces, feelings of compression coexist with passages of openness and airiness.

TERRY WINTERS, *Field of View,* 1993.
76 x 96 inches (193.1 x 243.9 cm).
Oil, alkyd resin on linen.
Photo by Steven Sloman.
Courtesy Matthew Marks Gallery,
New York, NY.

Of course, the two designs also have pronounced differences. One has to do with color. Winters's painting uses a broad range of color from all around the wheel, and most of the color is quite saturated. As a result, his painting is very lively, bold, and exceedingly dynamic. The color of Sekijima's design derives exclusively from the apricot fiber. The result is nearly monochromatic and uniformly neutral, contributing to a great sense of unity.

The second area of difference has to do with the nature and degree of depth in the two design spaces. Winters's space is two dimensional, but he creates the illusion of depth in a number of ways: larger linear movements appear to come forward while smaller/thinner ones seem to recede; warm colors come forward in contrast to cold greens, blues, and purples that recede; and some linear movements come forward as they overlap others. Sekijima's sculpture, on the other hand, has actual depth. Some fiber pieces exist literally in front of others. This sensation of depth is heightened by the shadows created by the forms. But because the actual depth here is quite shallow (approximately 3 inches [7.6 cm]) and because there are no color contrasts to push elements forward and back, Sekijima's composition feels shallower than it actually is. Consider which design you think has a feeling of greater depth, and why.

GLOSSARY OF DESIGN TERMS

A

Abstraction. The process of responding to a visual reference by selecting, exaggerating, distilling, or otherwise altering elements and arrangements to serve a variety of design purposes.

Acting and responding. An approach to design that emphasizes working with visual elements in an improvisational manner. The approach de-emphasizes planning and control in an effort to embrace the design process itself as subject.

Actual texture. The quality of a surface experienced through the sense of touch—smooth, gritty, slick, crinkled, bumpy, slimy, fuzzy, and so on.

Adjacent colors. Colors located next to or very near one another on the color wheel.

Aesthetics. The branch of philosophy related to the nature of beauty.

Atmospheric perspective. A system for creating the illusion of depth (three dimensions) in a two-dimensional design space. Dramatic visual contrasts create a sense of nearness while gradually decreasing contrasts create an increasing sense of distance.

B

Bilateral symmetry. A kind of balance that occurs when elements on one side of a single central axis are mirrored by like elements on the other side.

C

Color. The qualities of hue, value, saturation, and temperature observed in an experience of light reflected from a surface.

Complementary colors. Colors located opposite one another on the color wheel.

Composition. The arrangement of visual forces in space; synonymous with design.

Contour crosshatching. A specific kind of crosshatching in which both series of hatched lines run parallel with the edges of a shape or form, usually for the dual purposes of creating value and indicating form and direction.

Crosshatching. When one series of parallel lines intersects with a second series of parallel lines, usually for the purpose of creating value. All else being equal, the denser the crosshatching, the darker the value.

D

Decorative. The design purpose that seeks to adorn or to create a design that will serve as an object of meditation; design as subject.

Descriptive. The design purpose that seeks to convey the visible reality of a subject; synonymous with documentary.

Design. 1. (noun) An arrangement of visual elements in space. 2. (verb) To arrange visual elements in space.

Design space. The area that contains or frames an arrangement of visual elements; may be two dimensional (canvases, billboards, swatches of fabric, etc.) or three dimensional (blocks of wood, pieces of stone, slabs of clay, etc.).

Documentary. The design purpose that seeks to convey the visible reality of a subject; synonymous with descriptive.

E

Edge. The place where one shape butts up against another; the place where one shape of color stops and an adjacent one begins.

Emotive. The design purpose that seeks to evoke a mood or convey a feeling.

F

Focal point. The place of primary emphasis in a design; the first place the eye is drawn to in its experience of a design. Also serves as a place for the eye to return to and rest during its experience of a design.

Form. A three-dimensional area with identifiable boundaries; features dimensions of height, width, and depth.

Formal. The design purpose that seeks to create an arrangement to serve as an object of meditation; design as subject.

Fresco. A painting technique in which water media is applied to a moist plaster surface. When dry, the pigments become incorporated into the plaster surface itself.

Functional. The design purpose that seeks to fulfill a practical purpose; synonymous with utilitarian.

G

Geometric shapes. Shapes in the square-circle-triangle family, characterized by edges that are perfectly straight or curved; universally recognizable.

H

Hatching. A series of parallel lines, usually arranged for the purpose of creating value. All else being equal, the denser the hatching, the darker the value.

Hue. Color identity determined by the manner in which light is reflected from a surface.

I

Imaginary texture. When a series of two-dimensional visual elements (line, mark, texture, shape, or color) is arranged in a way that evokes a sense of touch.

Interval. An area or space that separates one element from the next in a rhythmic sequence.

L

Line. 1. The recorded movement of a dot on its journey from one place to another. 2. A mark the length of which is very much greater than its width.

M

Mandala. A design structure featuring radial symmetry, concentric geometrical shapes, and images of deities. In Hinduism and Buddhism, these designs represent the wholeness of the universe and serve as objects of meditation.

Mark. A visible impression left on a surface when touched by a tool or other object.

Modernism. A movement from the late 19th century through the 1960s that brought about radical changes in the purposes and mindset of making art. It's generally marked by concern with internal or spiritual realities rather than exterior ones, and by the elevation of design elements and the design process to subject-matter status.

Modified symmetry. 1. A kind of balance that occurs when elements on one side of a central axis are mirrored by similar elements in similar placements on the other side. 2. Symmetrical balance with subtle variations.

Monochromatic design. A design that exhibits little or no contrast in hue. Monochromatic arrangements may consist of any one color and its variations when mixed with white, black, or gray, or of white, black, and a series of grays in between.

Motif. A primary element in a design—most often a shape or color—that is repeated, elaborated on, or explored.

N

Narrative. The design purpose that seeks to tell a story, entertain, preach, educate, or comment.

Negative shape/space. An area that feels unoccupied or passive in relation to its surroundings.

Neutral color. A color such as black, white, gray, or brown not readily identifiable with one single hue; highly unsaturated color.

Nonobjective. Designs that are entirely without recognizable forms from nature.

O

Organic shape. A shape based on forms found in nature, most often rounded and irregular, or a shape that appears to have grown or evolved into being.

P

Pastel. A color to which white has been added, lightening it and robbing it of its intensity.

Pattern. Visual elements repeated in a coherent and orderly manner.

Perfect symmetry. 1. A kind of balance that occurs when elements on one side of a central axis are perfectly mirrored by identical elements on the other side. 2. Symmetrical balance with no variation.

Placement. The location and orientation of an element in relation to the outside parameters of a design space as well as to other elements in the space.

Positive shape/space. An area that feels occupied or activated in relation to its surroundings.

Primary color. One of the three pure hues—red, yellow, and blue—that are irreducible, meaning they can't be created by mixing other colors together.

R

Radial symmetry. A kind of balance that occurs when design elements mirror one another along numerous axes at the same time, and where the numerous axes intersect one another at a center point in the design space.

Representational. Designs that feature, to some degree, elements that read as recognizable forms from nature.

Rhythm. The sequential repetition of elements in a design; a patterned series of visual "beats" that speak to one another.

S

Saturation. The relative degree of purity a color exhibits. Highly saturated color is experienced as pure, full strength, rich; colors of low saturation are experienced as dull, diluted, spare.

Scale. The size (or area of coverage) of a visual element or cluster of elements in relation to its surroundings. Scale involves contrasts of big and small, monumental and intimate.

Secondary color. Color created when two primary colors are mixed to create a hue exactly halfway in between: orange (red and yellow), green (yellow and blue), and purple (blue and red).

Shape. A two-dimensional area with identifiable boundaries. Shape is characterized by height and width.

Simultaneous contrast. The optical phenomenon in which the experience of one color calls for the simultaneous experience of its complement. If the complement isn't present, the eye spontaneously creates the experience of it.

Symmetry. A kind of balance that occurs when elements on one side of a central axis or axes are mirrored by like elements on the other side. The axis or axes may run vertically, horizontally, or on a diagonal. See also perfect symmetry, modified symmetry, and radial symmetry.

T

Temperature. The relative degree of warmth and coolness associated with an experience of a color. Warmth is generally associated with colors in the red-orange-yellow family, while coolness is associated with colors on the green-blue-purple side of the color wheel.

Tertiary color. Color created when one primary color and one of its adjacent secondary colors are mixed to create a hue exactly halfway in between: red and orange make red orange, blue and green make blue green.

Three dimensional. An element or space characterized by height, width, and depth.

Transparency. The visual phenomenon that occurs when a relatively distant element or surface is visible through a relatively near one.

Trompe l'oeil. From the French for "fool the eye," trompe l'oeil is an arrangement of visual elements that is so convincingly descriptive it creates the illusion that a form or object actually exists.

Two dimensional. An element or space characterized by height and width.

U

Unity and variety. When design elements relate to one another with enough commonality to hold the space together and enough diversity to make things interesting.

Utilitarian. The design purpose that seeks to fulfill a practical purpose; synonymous with functional.

V

Value. The relative degree of light and dark associated with an experience of a tone or color, with black as the darkest, white the lightest, and middle-tone gray halfway in between.

Vessel. A shape or form that serves as a container for other elements or space.

Visual elements. The raw materials you use to design with: line, mark, texture, shape or form, and color.

W

Weighted line. A line that changes in thickness and presence as it moves on a journey from one point to another.

ACKNOWLEDGMENTS

My thanks to Rob Pulleyn, Carol Taylor, Deborah Morgenthal, and the rest of the decision-makers at Lark Books for affording me the opportunity to work from my strengths and passions in writing this book. Special thanks to Carol for embracing the project and for contributing insights that added exceptional focus and clarity.

I cannot offer enough in praise of my editor, Paige Gilchrist. She patiently nurtured and guided this process of "bookmaking" in every phase, every step of the way. She transformed my writing—which can at times be overly academic—into prose that is easy to read. Her organizational and interpersonal skills have made this project a joy to be a part of. In many ways, this book is as much hers as it is mine.

A book on design must be superbly composed, and this one is, thanks to art director Dana Irwin, an exceptionally accomplished designer and fine artist (Dana doubled as illustrator for the book). Her vision played an indispensable role in the creation of this book. It also needed a beautifully designed cover, and we have one, thanks to Barbara Zaretsky. Thanks, also, to production assistant Hannes Charen for working with me on the challenging task of creating color scales and grids.

Heartfelt thanks to associate editor Veronika Alice Gunter, who contributed an unusual combination of intelligent enthusiasm and nuts-and-bolts efficiency that helped keep the process of creating this book flowing. She also oversaw our photo acquisitions, a substantial task in a book of this kind. Following up on stellar work done early on by assistant editor Heather Smith, Veronika was magically able to acquire virtually all the imagery I requested, with the help of Nathalie Mornu and Cindy Burda. Thank you all for your tireless pursuit of images from a wide range of sources—your efforts help make this book so illuminating. Finally, thanks to Delores Gosnell and Rosemary Kast for their earnest, supportive contributions in the everyday processing of many tasks related to this book.

****

I am also indebted to many for their encouragement and support of my work over the years, among them: my parents, Ken and Ruth Aimone, and the rest of the Aimone family; Pope and Margaret Duncan; Stephen Palmieri; Gary and

Jane Bolding; Dan and Helen Wozniak; Betty Parker; Gertrude Riley; Louise and Mary Napolitano; Kathryn Markel; Paul Gianfagna; Laura Stewart; Jeannie Dowis; Chris Harris; and Charlene and Jim Thomas. My sincere appreciation, as well, to the student-artists at Stetson University and Western Carolina University.

Finally, a very special thanks to the rich and diverse community of second-career artists who have participated in my workshops over the years. You've confirmed for me that in design, as in life, there are limitless possibilities.

ABOUT THE AUTHOR

Steven Aimone holds an MFA in painting and drawing from Brooklyn College. He has gained a national reputation as a workshop teacher in the areas of design and painting through teaching professional artists, craftspeople, college students, and teachers. He has taught design workshops to a variety of groups—the Society of American Mosaic Artists, Tapestry Weavers South, MountainMade Foundation (based in West Virginia), and other professional art and craft groups.

He frequently serves as a lecturer on the subject of design at universities, colleges, and museums. He also does on-line coaching and critiques for artists and craftspeople, and he was a guest interviewee on this subject for an article published in *Fiberarts* magazine.

He teaches a series of workshops titled "The Spiritual Language of Art" at the prestigious Atlantic Center for the Arts in New Smyrna Beach, Florida. He also teaches an annual painting workshop every June on Monhegan Island, Maine. He and his wife Katherine run Aimone Art Services, their joint venture that offers art and design workshops along with writing and curatorial services. For more information, visit his website at www.aimoneartservices.com or write to him at info@aimoneartservices.com.

ARTIST INDEX

IMAGERY CREDITS

FRONT COVER:

CLOCKWISE FROM TOP LEFT: FRANZ KLINE, *Figure 8*, 1952. $80^7/_8$ x $63^3/_8$ (205.4 x 161 cm). Oil on canvas. Collection of Harry W. and Mary Margaret Anderson. **KYUNGAE JEON**, *Untitled*, 1998. Approx. 38 x 31 x 8 inches (97 x 79 x 20 cm). Cast and formed handmade flax-hemp paper over armature. **ELLEN MARSH AND ROBIN MCKAY**, *Magic Geometry in Natural (Transparencies Collection)*, 1998. Discharge paste printed, clamped, and resist dyed silk organza; black silk georgette tank dress. *Photo by Wit McKay.* **ERIC NELSEN**, *Traveler #25*, 1994. 27 x 22 x 10 inches (68.6 x 55.9 x 25.4 cm). Anagama fired clay; hand built, slab, coiling, thrown, press molded, carved, extruded. *Photo by Roger Schreiber.* **DEBRA STONER**, *Judy's Inheritance*, 1994. 5 x 5 x $1^1/_2$ (12.7 x 12.7 x 3.8 cm). Eyeglasses of steel, platinum, diamonds, lenses; fabricated. *Photo by Marcus Swanson.* **SUSIE PONDS**, *Green Snake Quilt*, 1979. 64 x 80 inches (162.6 x 203.2 cm). Quilted. From the collection of Maude and James Wahlman. *Originally published in Wahlman, Signs and Symbols.* **LARRY HOPKINS**, *Asian Fusion*, 2002. Hair design. Model: Kyoko Masukyo. *Photo by Kelly Giezentanner. Courtesy of Ananda Hair Studio, Asheville, NC.*

ROB PULLEYN, *Rock Wall*. Color photograph. **ELIZABETH MURRAY**, *Bowtie*, 2000. 85 x $77^1/_2$ inches (215.9 x 196.9 cm). Oil on canvas. Photo by Kerry R. McFate. *Courtesy of Pace Wildenstein © Elizabeth Murray.* **JUDY GLASSER**, *Carved Vase*, 1997. 12 x 15 x 6 inches (30.5 x 38.1 x 15.2 cm). Stoneware. *Photo by Theresa Schwiendt.* **CHARLES MANN**, *East Lambrook Garden*, 1991. Color photograph of a garden in Wiltshire, England. Garden designer: **MARJORIE FISH**. **FRED FENSTER**, *Teapot*, 1995. 11 x 6 x 5 inches (27.9 x 15.2 x 12.7 cm). Fabrication using pewter. *Photo by artist.*

HALF TITLE PAGE:

GIORGIO MORANDI, *Still Life*, 1968. 10 x 16 inches (25.4 x 40.6 cm). Oil on canvas. *Photo by Steve Tatum. Courtesy of University of Iowa Museum of Art, Iowa City, IA. (Gift of Owen and Leone Elliott, accession number 1968.36*

SANG PARKINSON-ROBERSON, *Untitled*, 2000. 8 x 8 x 6 inches (20.3 x 20.3 x 15.3 cm). Pit-fired terra cotta burnished with terra sigilatta; bound with waxed linen; carnelian stone on lid. *Photo by Tim Tew/Studio Tew.*

TITLE PAGE:

WAYNE THIEBAUD, *Around the Cake*, 1962. 22 x 28 inches (55.9 x 71.1 cm). Oil on canvas. *Spencer Museum of Art: The University of Kansas, Lawrence, KS. Gift of Ralph T. Coe in memory of Helen F. Spencer.*

TABLE OF CONTENTS:

EDWARD S. EBERLE, *Teapot Study*, 1992. 10 x $10^1/_2$ x $5^1/_4$ inches (25.4 x 26.7 x 13.3 cm). Terra sigilata on porcelain. *Photo by artist.*

DON GUREWITZ, *Granary*, 1999. Color photograph taken in Dogon country, Mali. *Collection of the artist.*

DEDICATION PAGE:

STEVEN AIMONE, *Black Mountain Compositions*, 2001. Each $11^1/_4$ x $11^1/_4$ x $1^1/_2$ (28.6 x 28.6 x 3.8 cm). Oil on wood. *Photo by Tim Barnwell.*

INDEX